GABRIEL FACKRE attended Bucknell University and received his Ph.D. from the University of Chicago Divinity School. In 1967-68 he was a Senior Research Fellow at Mansfield College, Oxford University. An ordained minister of the United Church of Christ, Dr. Fackre served two pastorates before joining the faculty of the Lancaster Theological Seminary, where he is a Professor of Theology and Culture. He is the author of eight other books and numerous articles which have appeared in such journals as *The Christian Century* and *Christianity and Crisis*.

The *Promise*
of
Reinhold Niebuhr

The Promise
of
Reinhold Niebuhr

by
GABRIEL FACKRE

J. B. LIPPINCOTT COMPANY
Philadelphia and New York

To James Luther Adams,

my other mentor

Foreword

No native-born American more readily became a candidate for inclusion in this series of books on futures than did Reinhold Niebuhr. For over a third of a century he has been a shaping influence in theology, social ethics and public policy. Those who speak in faintly condescending tones about other twentieth-century giants in religious thought, as if their days are past and their contributions forgotten, are more reluctant to do so when Niebuhr's name is brought up.

For one thing, the longtime Union Theological Seminary professor is a moving target. As both his biographer and Professor Fackre have pointed out, he has always had "the courage to change." Today's radicals cannot dismiss a man who so early saw prospects in Marxian thought. The people on the New Politics part of the spectrum cannot deny that he helped set a basis for them in his Christian realism. Main-line theologians applaud the way in which he was grounded in classical Christian themes, not even shunning some unpopular doctrines like "original sin." And even innocent bystanders live with policies developed by men who acknowledge that Niebuhr's thought informed theirs. Niebuhr has his enemies, too—another good sign that there is potency and promise in his thought.

Like most of the subjects of books in this series, Niebuhr has been a very productive man. Unlike many of them, he has not ordinarily chosen the systematic tome as the means of expressing himself—though *The Nature and Destiny of Man* towers in that category. To approach Niebuhr one must read thousands of editorials and short articles, cope with impressive sermons, tie together themes from many short occasional books. Fackre has done this and presents readers with a coherent view of Niebuhr, accenting the themes that now have to be wrestled with more than others, themes which suggest some directions theology and Christian action could well take today.

MARTIN E. MARTY
The University of Chicago

Contents

Introduction

Hard-nosed radicals are telling us these days that we must learn again to daydream. To build a castle in the air is to refuse to take with absolute seriousness things as they are, says the renegade Marxist, Ernst Bloch. The visionary is the revolutionary; his loyalty is to the future, not the present. In very different idiom, Herman Kahn sketches scenarios of things to come. Even this "futurology" with its think-tanks funded by the powers that be can have its radical edge, as it calls for efforts to disprove the nightmares and fulfill the dreams. Then too there are those gentle visionaries, the youth counter-culture whose flower power, communes and psychedelics celebrate the coming of the age of Aquarius. And now, on top of all this, accents are being heard in Christian thought that stress the Not Yet. "Eschatology," that doctrine with its heady hopes for a new future, comes center stage. Alongside this theology of hope stands a theology of revolution, the restless urge to bend the givens into pointers to Kingdom Come.

What does Reinhold Niebuhr have to say to an era whose secular and theological pacemakers talk of revolutionary hope? Do his somber reports of history's ambiguities and man's sin have any relevance to a time when young men see visions and old men dream dreams? Is Christian realism a blind alley for a period that needs to hear of the race's possibilities rather than its impossibilities?

A case could be made that both ends of the theological foundation of another era, biblical realism, are eroding. On the one hand, the "biblical" rootage comes under attack from those whose point of reference is the secular experience of the present, rather than the "mighty acts" of the religious past. Former Niebuhrians proclaim their disillusionment with penumbras of mystery and announce the death of God. On the other hand, revolutionary futurists with their theology of hope bring "realism" under sharp attack. They point to disciples of Niebuhr who have translated his thought into mild establishment-oriented efforts at reform and joined the resistance to an adventuresome New Left politics and religion. They tell us men aspiring for a fuller life must not be immobilized by talk of tainted motives, but turned on by whetted expectations; not reproached for privateering, but sprung loose from lassitude, and toward radical social change. Hope, not sin, is the great new word. Where, they ask, can these sounds be heard in a Niebuhrian vocabulary?

A book on the promise of Reinhold Niebuhr will struggle with that kind of question. We will review the highlights of his life and thought, but it will not be a detailed or a full-orbed reportage. Read Gordon Harland's *The Thought of Reinhold Niebuhr,* Kegley and Bretall's *Reinhold Niebuhr,* or June Bingham's *Courage to Change* for perceptive and comprehensive probings of that sort.[1]* Here we try to take seriously the special purpose of this series by asking what in Niebuhr's thought needs to be preserved or resurrected for us, or rejected by us, in the midst of our present theological urges and political surges. And we shall not denigrate the "theological" Niebuhr, as some are prone to do who see his contribution to be primarily in the political, or, at best, social ethical, arena. In fact, as befits a series on great theologians, we shall concentrate on the exposure of the doctrinal foundations crucial for the building of future faith and action.

While never a student of Niebuhr's, I was profoundly influenced by him in vocation as well as theology, testing the theses of Christian realism in a ten-year parish ministry

---

*Superior figures refer to the Notes at the end of the text.

among Pittsburgh steelworkers and their families, before teaching in a seminary. This inquiry comes very close to home, therefore, especially as I am drawn toward a theology of hope, some of whose exponents raise serious questions about the continuing relevance of realism. One of the personal fruits of the study is the conviction that it is folly to polarize realism and vision. Current theology, church life and political ferment, with their dreams, celebrations and hopes, desperately need the insights of Reinhold Niebuhr. And there is more ore to be mined in this mountainous thinker than that derived from the realism-hope debate, as we shall explore in the final chapter. In reviewing his career, therefore, we shall examine not only the skeletal facts but fix, as well, upon a life-style from which we can learn. And in lifting up the motifs in his theology, ethics and political thought, there will be focus on those aspects that afford clues to doing theology and being in mission, today and tomorrow.

I

The Life and Style of Reinhold Niebuhr

Someone has observed that there are in America more doctoral dissertations about Niebuhr than any other twentieth-century theologian. And the library card files are fat with books analyzing him. Every canyon and crevice of his story has been explored, including the paths of his intellectual and personal pilgrimage. With our promissory purpose in mind, we are more interested, in this biographical chapter, in tracing the lineaments of a style of life that have something to say to us, rather than simply repeating data about him.

The Early Years

Karl Paul Reinhold Niebuhr was born in Wright City, Missouri, June 21, 1892, to parents who were serving a German-speaking congregation in the small Evangelical Synod, which mixed the Lutheran and Reformed traditions. The Reverend Gustav Niebuhr and his wife, Lydia, had other children—Helmut Richard, who is honored in the Promise series as another outstanding Christian thinker; Hulda, who also entered the lists as a theologian, teaching and writing for many years at McCormick Theological Seminary in Chicago; Walter, a pioneering publisher and businessman; and Hubert, who died as an infant. Reinhold Niebuhr frequently expressed his gratitude for the security, love and openness of his family life years. While discipline was not absent, Pastor Niebuhr had left his homeland in protest of Prussian rigidities, and therefore added warmth and give-and-take to the family life-style.

"Reinie" grew up in Missouri and Illinois parsonages. The environment had its impact, for one day he announced that his father was the "most interesting man in town." It came as no surprise, therefore, that he gravitated toward the professional ministry, entering the Evangelical Synod's Elmhurst College in suburban Chicago, then going on to Eden Theological Seminary in Webster Groves, Missouri. His academic achievements and eagerness to break loose from the tight web of German church life pressed him to continue his studies at Yale for another few years, earning a B.D. and an M.A. His keen mind carved out a respected niche for himself among the Ivy League sophisticates. The renowned exponent of evangelical liberalism, Douglas Clyde Macintosh, exercised a particularly strong influence on him, although professor and student had animated exchanges on their differences at Yale and in later years.

Commitments to the church and a certain fatigue with prolonged intellectual incubation led Niehbuhr to accept the pastorate of a small congregation in Detroit, to which he moved in 1915. As his father had died in 1913, his mother accompanied him to the new charge.

1915 to 1928: Detroit

Niebuhr launched his ministry in the company of the eighteen families of Bethel Evangelical Church, "the little German church around the corner." A Detroit population explosion, powerful preaching, and the dedicated organizational labors of Mrs. Lydia Niebuhr sent the membership to nearly seven hundred and put the congregation in an imposing new building over the period of his thirteen-year ministry. But these figures are not the heart of the matter.

In Detroit, Niebuhr was beginning to find out about industrial America. His congregation was a cross-section of metropolis, running from a sprinkling of wage workers through a varied middle-class majority to a few millionaires. His pastoral rounds and civic activities brought him in contact with the unemployed, those retired at the height of their working powers because of the automobile industry's age policies, and those broken suppliers to, and competitors of, the giant of the industry—Ford. Henry Ford had a world reputation, not only as a technological innovator but also as a humanitarian, trailing behind him a well-publicized record of high wages, the five-day week and hiring the handicapped. It was in the close-up view of the human ravages left by big business that Niebuhr's social conscience and realism took form.

Behind the "high wages" lay Ford's high profits. And behind that was a production genius which included efficiency-engineered speedups, model changeover, retooling with its long factory shutdowns and mass layoffs, a Charlie Chaplin assembly-line life, the shelving of aged workers and an anti-union policy. Niebuhr's response to industrial dehumanization ran the gamut from personal ministry to public protest. He sought to find jobs for individual castoffs; he welcomed representatives of labor into his church to tell their story in the face of sharp protests by the Detroit Board of Commerce; he helped found the Emergency Committee for Strike Relief; he filed periodic reports with *The Christian Century* on the machinations of the automobile industry, to the vocal displeasure of Ford enterprises. This on-location exposure to the gap between the pretension and performance of an industrial barony contributed to Niebuhr's realism, particularly regarding collectivities. Further, tirades directed initially at Ford developed into more sophisticated analyses of structural weaknesses in the economy that later took shape as an attack on capitalism.

Detroit was a laboratory in racial learning as well as labor conflict. With the supply of European immigrants cut off by the war, the automobile industry drew large numbers of black citizens from the South. Niebuhr was among the

[17]

church leadership that early participated in their struggle for basic justice, serving as the first chairman of a Mayor's Commission on Racial Relations and taking controversial stands on specific issues of racial injustice. His congregation had a self-declared open membership policy, with four or five Negro families attending services, though none joined.

Niebuhr's parish ministry fell in the period of the "Great War." He served as a member of a denominational commission that visited many of the stateside army camps, and in 1919 he went on an inspection tour of the Ruhr with YMCA leader Sherwood Eddy, the reports of which stirred the government to take relief action. While going along initially with American participation in the war, and expressing regrets to his Yale classmates at not being able to be a chaplain, Niebuhr became more and more disillusioned with that venture, in particular, and war in general. In 1923 he became a declared pacifist and several years later was an active member of the Fellowship of Reconciliation (FOR).

Niebuhr's involvement in economic, social and political affairs was influenced to no small extent by prophetic figures on the Detroit scene. One of them was Episcopal Bishop Charles Williams. While other clergymen ran for cover in controversy, Williams consistently supported worker rights, justice for blacks and peace movements. He stood as proof to Niebuhr that the church could still produce an Amos. And, echoing Williams, he learned that in matters of social witness, the biblical position was often represented more faithfully by heirs of the prophets in the Jewish community, such as Detroit's Fred Butzell, than those in the church. This early comradeship with latter-day Amoses was to be a constant in Niebuhr's later political involvements and in his views on Jewish-Christian relations.

While the prophetic figured prominently in Niebuhr's Detroit ministry, he was also a pastor attentive to the needs of the members of his congregation. His reflection on the tragedy and joys of his parishioners in *Leaves from the Notebook of a Tamed Cynic* (1929), as well as their own testimony, reveals a sensitivity to the claims of the personal life and a faithfulness to individual Christian ministrations. In later years Niebuhr expressed regret that in the midst of his busy public life he could not have given even more attention to the tender and intimate dimensions of ministry.

The association and friendship with Sherwood Eddy drew Niebuhr into the orbit of national life. Eddy opened the way for him to a larger audience by helping to provide funds for an assistant at Bethel Church so that the growing number of invitations to speak at colleges could be met. Thus began the circuit-riding that took Niebuhr to hundreds of centers of higher education in the years to come. Plunging him further into the national arena was the request by social reformer Jane Addams to assist in the 1926 presidential campaign of Robert LaFollette. Meanwhile Niebuhr was also writing for *The Atlantic Monthly* and *The Christian Century* (serving for a while on its editorial staff), and he produced his first book, *Does Civilization Need Religion?*, in 1927.

As Niebuhr increasingly moved in circles beyond his local parish, the logic of a platform commensurate with this audience asserted itself. In 1928 he accepted a teaching post at Union Theological Seminary in New York City. As well as being at a central point for forming the Protestant mind, he would be positioned at the crossroads of American intellectual and political ferment, and where the traffic from European church life also flowed. These factors exercised a significant influence on Niebuhr's subsequent life-style.

1929 to 1945: From Depression to Conflagration

Seminary life allowed for, and demanded, more rigorous intellectual confrontation with the human issues Niebuhr had lived with in Detroit. He read Karl Marx and came in touch with the currents of radical social criticism. On top of that were poured more data from the economic cataclysm of 1929 and its sequel, a hungry and despairing America. In the pages of *World Tomorrow,* an organ of the Fellowship of Reconciliation, and in such landmark volumes of the thirties as *Moral Man and Immoral Society* (1932), *Reflections on the End of an Era* (1934) and *An Interpretation of Christian Ethics* (1935), capitalism was pinpointed as the source of our social sickness and Roosevelt's New Deal was dismissed as a mild injection that dulled the patient's awareness of approaching death.

At the opening of the decade Niebuhr nailed down his anticapitalist commitments as a leading spirit in the founding of the Fellowship of Socialist Christians and the editing of its periodical, *Radical Religion.* He joined the Socialist Party and appeared on its ballot as a congressional candidate from a local New York district in 1930. He became a familiar figure in radical circles as he lived out his declaration to "move politically to the left and theologically to the right."

It was that latter mobility, "theologically to the right," which distinguished him from many who had made the pilgrimage to radicalism in the depressed thirties. The theological right meant a biblical realism which wound itself into the socialist motifs. On the one hand, it pressed him to the left of a mild social protest which was confident of man's goodness, the methods of moral suasion and education, and history's escalation upward. On the other, it led him to reject the utopianism of the orthodox Marxist, which claimed to have seen and secured the future and expressed itself in the fanaticism of a Stalinist purge or the mindless rigidity of the American Communist Party. For that reason he was found regularly in the first ranks of antiestablishment activists who at the same time carried on a second front against Marxist ideologues seeking to gain control of reform movements. This double battle he waged in such groups as the New York Teachers' Union and other New York and national movements.

Toward the end of the decade, Niebuhr's attention turned increasingly to the issues of war and peace. Having served for several years in earlier pacifist days as chairman of the FOR, he now began to grapple with the Nazi phenomenon. He had laid down the main lines of his criticism of pacifism in *An Interpretation of Christian Ethics*. As Hitler rattled German sabers more loudly, and as the horrible fate of the Jew broke into the consciousness of the world, Niebuhr became an increasingly outspoken critic of appeasement. A peripatetic teaching that frequently took him to Europe, his personal friendship with such expatriates as theologian Paul Tillich and social philosopher Eduard Heimann, and leaders in the Christian resistance movement like Dietrich Bonhoeffer brought home to him the price being paid by inaction and dramatized, as well, the challenge to the church of the Nazis' "blood and soil" racism. While Neibuhr did not plead radical intervention in terms of troops and a declaration of war until 1941, he backed many causes that aided refugees and supported the Allies materially, including the protection of cargo shipments.

As the antipacifist posture accelerated, so did the disengagement from the movements of another era whose commitments seemed obsolete. In 1940 Niebuhr resigned from the Socialist Party, over its international policies, and later helped to found the Liberal Party. As the Soviet bear and its American cubs gave off very ambiguous noises about the Nazis in this period, he also took part in the organization of the Union for Democratic Action (UDA) in 1940, which sought to gather reformers around a common banner that excluded the communist doctrinaire.

Keeping under critical review the contest among the major political options—a very imperfect form of Western democracy, an all-out attack on the charter of human society itself (Nazism), and a too-easy formulation of a new humanism with its demonic possibilities (Marxism)—he was compelled to make the realignments just cited and more like them. This meant, for example, developing working relationships with the breed he had dismissed heretofore as committed to palliatives. Thus, Mrs. Franklin Delano Roosevelt, Elmer Davis and others in left-wing Democratic Party activities became his close associates. It also meant access to the Luce publications and other major media. Although Niebuhr's still strong "politically to the left" leanings were hardly the company policy of *Life* and *Time*, his anti-Nazi posture and some of his theological insights were attractive to them. Moreover, the media could hardly mute the message of one who was taking on international prominence as a molder of opinion. It meant also the beginning of a long association with government policy-makers, in particular in the State Department, whose public statements sometimes bore an almost embarrassing similarity to Niebuhrian concepts and language. In this period of changing loyalties and associations, many of his co-workers in the Fellowship of Christian Socialists followed suit. And the temperature change itself in this circle was signaled by an organizational nomenclature shift to the Frontier Fellowship and, finally, to Christian Action.

Niebuhr's extensive writing in this period ran from the astute political commentary of the early *Moral Man and Immoral Society,* to later essays in *The Nation, The New Republic, Harper's, Life* and in his own publication, *Christianity and Crisis* (successor to *Radical Religion*), to probing theological analyses in media as varied as the editorial pages of the Evangelical and Reformed *Messenger* and the massively researched two-volume *The Nature and Destiny of Man* (1941, 1943). This latter classic was given against the backdrop of Edinburgh air raid sirens, as the Gifford Lectures of 1939-1940. This statement of the Christian doctrine of man marked Niebuhr (despite his own disclaimers to be a theologian) as one of the most fertile theological minds of the twentieth century. Paralleling the more formal academic and political commentary was the continuing flow of sermons and addresses which found their way into such collections as *Beyond Tragedy* (1937) and *Discerning the Signs of the Times* (1946).

While the life of the mind and the struggle of nations occupied much of Niebuhr's attention during these years, there was a time for tender things as well. He has often remarked that without the latter there would have been few resources for the former. Vivacious Oxford honor student Ursula Keppel-Compton came to Union Seminary in the fall of 1930. Niebuhr married her in 1931. The relationship has had its intellectual electricity as well as its warm personal dimensions. Mrs. Niebuhr, demonstrating her own theological alertness through her teaching at Barnard (ultimately heading the department of religion), has proved to be one of the most astute critics of her husband's thought, influencing him significantly, as he testified in later years.

The Niebuhr home came to be not only the center of a lively family circle, adding Christopher and Elizabeth in subsequent years, but also a house of hospitality for students who looked forward to the once-a-week evening living room dialogues. A number of strong friendships between the Niebuhrs and such intellectual and religious leaders as Will Herberg, Bishop William Scarlett and others also flowered in the more private circle of Niebuhrian life.

The familial is not often recognized as an important ingredient in the prophetic. Neither is the devotional. Yet it was out of Niebuhrian spirituality that a prayer took form on a summer Sunday in 1934 destined to be used by chaplains and sufferers in countless hospital rooms and on battlefields, and adopted as the official prayer of Alcoholics Anonymous. "O God, give us serenity to accept what cannot be changed, courage to change what should be changed, and wisdom to distinguish the one from the other." While rarely vocal on a subject scarred by sentimentality, Niebuhr knew as a pastor, and later in the feverish thirties and forties when exhaustion from overwork felled him at several critical junctures, something of the sustenance and celebration that comes with "friendship with God."

1945 to 1960: The Postwar Years

Niebuhr's reorientation to a posture that sought to work within the framework of major political options was crystallized in 1947 when he assisted in the formation of Americans for Democratic Action, a more broad-based growth from UDA, independent in its party commitments but, in effect, a left-wing gadfly within the Democratic Party. With its non-Communist declaration, it distinguished itself from such parallel developments as the Progressive Citizens of America, which supported the Henry Wallace presidential candidacy in 1948. This experience, and his growing stature as a political philosopher, drew Niebuhr further into the orbit of major American leadership as a consultant. The list of those who later sponsored a social ethics chair at Union Seminary bearing his name is an index of that influence. It included: Adolph Berle, Chester Bowles, Ralph Bunche, David Dubinsky, Norman Thomas, George Kennan, Paul Hoffman, Walter Reuther, Herbert Lehman, Walter Lippmann, Stanley Isaacs, Henry Luce, Arthur Schlesinger, Jr., Robert Oppenheimer, Eleanor Roosevelt, Beardsley Ruml, George Shuster, William Hocking, Adlai Stevenson, Charles Taft, Joseph Rauh, Hubert Humphrey and Robert Hutchins. World figures numbered in this group were Arnold Toynbee, Alan Paton, Barbara Ward, Jacques Maritain, Sir Sarvepalli Radhakrishnan, Sir Walter Moberly, W. H. Auden and Charles Malik.

Balancing the secular involvements were Niebuhr's associations in world Christianity. He had taken an active part in the ecumenical conversations on the relation of church to society at Oxford in 1937. Niebuhr played a further role at the first assembly of the World Council of Churches in Amsterdam in 1948, writing resource material and providing sectional leadership. He also exchanged literary volleys with Karl Barth about the Council theme on the Lordship of Christ, defending its quest for solutions to the intricate problems of the day against allegations that such efforts represent Atlas-like pretentions. He continued to serve as consultant to the National Council of Churches on current events, having been on its wartime commission "to establish a just and lasting peace," working with (and not infrequently in opposition to) Secretary of State John Foster Dulles.

[24]

In the postwar period of ecclesiastical expansionism, peace-of-mind cults and popular piety, Niebuhr exposed both the cheap grace in the formulas of Billy Graham and Norman Vincent Peale and the introversion of the religious establishment. Although his sharpest barbs were reserved for fellow churchmen, his warfare with secular delusions never relented. For example, he saw in Alfred Kinsey and his widely publicized sex research an illustration of naturalistic presuppositions about man (the equation of human sexuality with orgasm) which skewed his findings and gave less than reliable guidance for dealing with a strong biological impulse that in man was uniquely interwoven with subtler dimensions of personhood.

Some of those criticized by Niebuhr declined to engage in direct debate (Graham, Kinsey, Erich Fromm), but a lively give-and-take with others did go on in the pages of ecclesiastical and secular journals. Niebuhr acknowledges that a shift in his own thinking began to take place as a result of these dialogues and other influences. One important change is detectable in Niebuhr's employment of the doctrine of original sin. Feeling that a heavy use of biblical symbols and language with their antiquated and parochial associations was an impediment to interpreting the "truth in the myth," he increasingly shed the distinctively Christian imagery in his interpretation of man's self-regarding inclinations. Associated with this was the general softening of his former "homiletical polemics" against modern culture, and a growing attempt to discern the traces of creativity in it and in human relationships in general. He never ceased, of course, to pinpoint the ambiguities and idolatries which persist in and pervade human experience. While continuing to take his own stand in the mainstream Reformation tradition, Niebuhr stressed with growing vigor the contributions of other religious traditions. Always affirmative of prophetic Judaism, he went further in the fifties to declare that the church should not attempt to convert Jews to the Christian faith, concentrating rather on a penitent exorcism of its age-old anti-Semitism, and an appropriation of the passion for social justice of the prophets. Niebuhr, a persistent critic of Roman Catholic cultural and doctrinal rigidity, also expressed a growing appreciation for its insights and new evidences of flexibility especially manifest in the Second Vatican Council and its liberating consequences in many sectors of the Church. In particular Niebuhr acknowledged in 1969 a new appreciation for the "intellectual, theological and moral creativities of the Jesuits."[1]

Niebuhr continued to be a major figure on the Union Seminary faculty (appointed later vice-president as well as professor of social ethics), and engaged in friendly running debates with colleagues Paul Tillich, John Bennett and Henry Pitney van Dusen. With its potent combination of biblical commitment and social and political action, Christian realism began to make its presence felt in the appearance of a new breed of church leader, the theologian, pastor, church executive, missionary and layman influenced to one extent or another by Niebuhrian themes. Representative of these various types were men like Roger L. Shinn, who succeeded Niebuhr at Union in the chair of Applied Christianity; George William Webber, founder of the East Harlem Protestant Parish and later president of New York Biblical Seminary; Truman Douglass, leading spirit in the affairs of the National Council of Churches and pioneer in church involvement in human issues; and Martin Luther King, Jr., who in a BBC interview shortly before his death described Niebuhr and Gandhi as the major intellectual influences in his life.

In the midst of the joys of a growing family and a lively conjugal partnership, the postwar period brought with it serious personal stresses and strains. Niebuhr underwent treatment for a critical brain illness and after extended hospitalization was forced to curtail his activities for many months. While gaining back most of the use of his speech and some of his arm movement, he was not able to undertake the globe-trotting and extensive writing projects of former days. Along with the physical hardships of this time, Niebuhr testified to a spiritual depression which normally accompanies the kind of brain impairment he experienced. The time for reflection and the thoughts generated in this setting prompted Niebuhr to search more deeply into the dynamics of selfhood and the significance of the intimate sectors and interpersonal aspects of human existence. That rumination is reflected in some of his writings of the period, such as *The Self and the Dramas of History* (1955).

While the private clamored for neglected attention, the public was far from forgotten. As noted earlier, association with political molders and shakers was a constant in his life. His books and periodical commentary showed too where his major interests now lay, in the field of political encounter and especially that of international affairs. From *The Children of Light and the Children of Darkness* (1944), through *The Structure of Nations and Empires* (1959), to *Faith and Politics* (1968), and in *Christianity and Crisis* editorials in the same period, Niebuhr's fertile mind was exercised with national and global developments. His *Faith and History* (1949) was a mark of his effort to blend theological and political interests, but in subsequent years the latter came increasingly to the fore.

1960 to the Present: Creative Retirement

Although formal relinquishment of responsibilities at Union Seminary came in 1960, it is difficult to draw a neat retirement line in the life of Niebuhr. His services have been sought out by the Institute for Advanced Studies in Princeton, and he has been active in the Center for the Study of Democratic Institutions at Santa Barbara, California. He served as well as a consultant, if not guru, for countless political and theological inquiries in the years after formal classroom teaching. While he left behind him the Riverside Heights apartment for the quieter life of Stockbridge, Massachusetts, in 1966, friends, visitors and interviewers continued their pilgrimage there, and correspondence and writings proceeded at a restricted but nonetheless sprightly pace.

In the 1960's Niebuhr wrote perceptively about issues in both church and world. Long anguished by the "American dilemma" and involved in ministry to it from the days in Detroit, participation in a Mississippi Delta cooperative and the founding of the Fellowship of Southern Churchmen in the thirties, he was heartened by the civil rights movement of the sixties, giving it his enthusiastic support.

On the international scene he was an early opponent, together with Hans Morgenthau, a longtime associate, of the Vietnam war (although not early enough for some of Niebuhr's critics). In a 1969 interview with one of his young interpreters, Ronald Stone, who edited *Faith and Politics,* Niebuhr gave some astute observations on the current issues of domestic and international concern.[2] Political commentary continued in such studies as *A Nation So Conceived* (1963) and *Man's Nature and His Communities* (1965).

Niebuhr never lacked for opponents. However, he was getting a new kind in this period, including those to both his right and left who were nursed on Niebuhrian themes. Either they bent them in a conservative direction or actively rebelled against formerly espoused postulates. Thus Will Herberg, Drew University professor of religion, a close friend and interpreter of an earlier Niebuhr, now is numbered among the writers for William Buckley's *National Review,* and Robert Fitch, social ethics faculty member at the Pacific School of Religion, launches diatribes against innovators in theology, morality and mission. Meanwhile, William Hamilton, a leading exponent of the "death of God" theology, expresses regret over his earlier captivity to Niebuhrian emphases.

The most sustained and carefully worked-out departure from early discipleship is found in the political critique of which Richard Shaull is the most forceful interpreter. Receptive to the thrust of the New Left, and supporter and interpreter of revolutions in the Third World (he served as missionary in Latin America for twelve years), Shaull believes that the symbols which served Niebuhr so well in illuminating another era of history do not make contact with our time. He holds that Niebuhrian realism settles its adherents too comfortably into the establishment, blunts the edge of radical social criticism needed today, and silences the notes of man's possibilities and hopes.[3]

Niebuhr continues in a limited way the conversation with his critics, taking exception to the "death of God" theology's insensitivity to mystery, grieving at rightist applications of his thoughts, and continuing to affirm the relevance of realism, yet with increasing accent on the possibilities of history, a theme that was always latent in his thoughts. However, it has been through the work of such interpreters as John Bennett and Roger Shinn that the dialogue continues with the new theologians of revolution and hope.[4]

Elements in the Niebuhrian Style of Life

From this rapid overview of Niebuhr's life, five characteristics stand out as life-style components that ought to make their contribution to our generation. Some already have done so.

1. Long before it became stylish to speak of "action research" or the "engagement-reflection methodology" on the campus or in Christian education circles, Reinhold Niebuhr was working out his theories in the context of practice. He "did" his theology in the setting of the pressing human issues of his day. His Christian realism was hammered out in the midst of his participation in the struggles against political, economic and social tyranny. As there could be no divorce of God from the world in his theology, so, in life-style, act was wedded to thought.

2. Niebuhr anticipated and gave impetus to the rediscovery by churchmen of "the secular." He saw Christian vocation to be in the midst of the human community, not in

flight from it. Not only his politics but also his Christian apologetic in sociological, philosophical and psychological idiom brought him into constant contact with those outside the Christian community, including many alien to any religious organization or profession. He joyfully affirmed the good things he saw in them, turned his heavy guns on the church for its failure to approach their level of insight or commitment, and allied himself in their causes for intellectual advance and social justice. He lost no time, as well, in exploding their illusions and pretensions.

3. Niebuhr's ministry found its center of gravity in the seminary, not the university. Together with his early pastorate, his service to denominational and ecumenical agencies points to a kind of involvement that took seriously the church as well as the world, and acted from within the faith community. A prophet he was to a rebellious people, and, like his biblical forebears who had a lover's quarrel with the covenant community, he was a "critic-in-residence."

4. His participation in public institutions was buttressed by a warm and deep personal and interpersonal life. Graced by a sustaining family in his earlier years, Niebuhr sought and found in his adulthood the supportive community of wife and children which embodied the I and Thou themes of Martin Buber, to which he was drawn in his theology. The wide circle of students, former students and compatriots in church and secular activity represented yet another expression of a style which thrived on the communal and contributed to it. And at the profoundest level of the intimate, in introspective analysis and prayer, Niebuhr, like one of his mentors, Augustine, was an explorer of the hidden heights and depths.

5. He has been free from captivity to the givens. This freedom is part of what June Bingham in her biography calls "the courage to change." Others describe it as pragmatism. But it is more than openness to correction, or adaptability. Niebuhrian freedom is the refusal to be caught on the horns of the conventional dilemmas, to be put in the box of pre-

dictable alternatives and constructs. Niebuhr was free enough to move theologically to the right and politically to the left, to defend the paradox when others could only see the orthodox, to discover the maneuvering room between doctrinaire options, to move in fresh and unforeseen ways beyond rigid polarities. Perhaps this can best be described as a freedom for the future, a quality much coveted in times oriented to the "not yet."

II

Theological Roots

Sometimes it is said that Niebuhr is really not a theologian but a political analyst, or at best a moralist. Such an observation may reveal more about the observer than Niebuhr, suggesting a point of view that divorces theory from practice. But more, it ignores the deep and massive roots of Christian reflection from which Niebuhr's political acumen and action spring. True, they are not set forth in the conventional categories of the systematician. But they are there. We shall try now to penetrate this rich subsurface. To do justice to its every twist and turn is an impossible goal for a single chapter. At best, we can only hope to discern its outlines and direction.

The center of Niebuhr's thought is anthropology, his understanding of who man is and where he is headed. The most extended diagnosis of these questions is found in his Gifford Lectures, *The Nature and Destiny of Man*, but it runs as well through all his works and is implicit in every observation he has made on the passing scene. Characteristically, his teaching emerged in the midst of a struggle with other options, particularly those with political implications and constituencies. We find our way into his thought through that turbulence and the great cultural premises that agitated it.

Twin Errors: Naturalism and Idealism

The anthropological illusions of a secular society are the source of its social disasters. Modern culture is of a divided mind on the question of man. Its miscalculations come in two basic varieties: naturalism and idealism.

Naturalism is struck by the affinities between man and his natural incubator. Man is a creature of his genes, his urges, his sensory input. Such a view comes in many sizes and shapes. It may explain our behavior in terms of body chemistry, hereditary predispositions, psychological forces, racial, sexual and age factors, climate, geography, economic and social impulses and conditioning, or combinations thereof. The self is seen, at the most, as conscious subject determined by internal and external forces, or, at the least, as a simple object in nature's chain of cause and effect. Talk of an "I" free to shape its future is illusory. Naturalism is as skeptical about a unity of human consciousness as it is about a cosmic Self.

Within the presuppositions of naturalism two modern versions stand out prominently: the empirical and the romantic. The former believes that man must learn to live by nature's laws, discerned by the scientific method. The latter, in flight from the corruptions of reason, counsels immersion in the passions and innocencies of nature.

Idealism locates the essence of man in a transnatural capacity, primarily the quality of reason. Its rationalist perspective is characterized by two assumptions. For one, it draws a sharp line between body and mind. A dualism of this sort denies the organic relation between thought and extension that characterizes naturalism. Secondly, idealism identifies virtue with reason and evil with the passions of nature. To cure human ills, it proposes to activate reason and slough off the inertias of man's animality.

Niebuhr traces in considerable detail the lively dynamics within and between these types, noting classic and modern developments, nuances, inconsistencies, interactions and their social effects. For example, he believes that individuality tends to be destroyed by both naturalism and idealism. Thus the former in its nineteenth-century romantic phase began by affirming the person in his uniqueness. But it evolved toward stress upon the individuality of the state, a thesis which prepared the way for the totalitarian brutalities of the twentieth-century. Idealism, which discovers dimensions of self unknown to naturalism and therefore knows something of human particularity, finally annihilates individuality in an abstract universalism. It also plays its own role, via Hegel's deification of the state as the historical expression of universal mind, in laying the groundwork for later movements of national self-glorification.

Both anthropologies have a high opinion of man and are confident of his future. Man's reason or his natural vitalities are to be trusted and will soar if the drags and lags can be eliminated. Each point of view finds particular institutions as the embodiment of man's defiance of nature or reason's laws. The conclusion is drawn, therefore, that the elimination of priestcraft, tyrannical government, an oppressive class or faulty economic organization, or inept education will solve the human problem.

Each asserts that the evidence for such an ascent is in the making. There is an immanent force at work in history (material or biological according to naturalism, and rational according to idealism) that guarantees upward movement. Society has progressed, and it can and will flow toward its fulfillment.

Niebuhr believes that these conceptions of man do not square with the facts as they can be perceived by human experience in its widest sense, nor do they provide an adequate basis for responsible personal and social living. We shall explore in more detail the tools Niebuhr uses to discriminate between true and false readings of the human situation. For the time being, we simply note that the options of modern culture prove futile in the long run.

But there is another choice. It is variously described as that of prophetic religion, biblical religion, high religion, the Judeo-Christian tradition, the Christian faith or the Hebraic strain. This alternative illumines man's choices and can be validated by our common experience, although commitment to it comes only through the act of penitence and faith and not by argumentation. This option saves from pretension, complacency and naïveté on the one hand, and despair and flight from the human struggle on the other. We shall attempt to describe it in terms of the dimensions, dynamics and destiny of man.

The Dimensions of Man

In contrast to naturalistic and idealistic reductionisms, Niebuhr describes man in a now-famous phrase as one who "lives at the juncture of nature and spirit." He is neither animal nor angel, but a unique amalgam of both. Let us look at the components in their interrelationships.

Man as Animal. As the naturalists rightly insist, man is intimately linked to the physico-biological matrix from which he springs. He is "subject to its vicissitudes, compelled by its necessities, driven by its impulses, confined within the brevity of the years which nature permits."[1] He is born of woman and marked by hereditary strain, is as dependent on parent as any animal, must eat, be protected from the elements, urinate, defecate, inhabit space, socialize, procreate and die. He is subject to conditioning from outside and drives from within. He is, therefore, "lived" by nature.

Man Is More. But nature is also "lived" by him. Man is conditioned but not programmed. A tiny control tower of spirit thrusts itself above the conditioning factors. From that perch the self looks down on its immersion in natural processes and seeks to bring some coherence and direction to the ebb and flow.

One of the notable dimensions of spirit is reason—the *nous, logos, ratio* that so captured the attention of Greek culture and since has been the distinguishing feature of man for rationalists. Reason is man's capacity to form general concepts. As thinking animal, man employs the instrument of

[35]

logic to sort out the stimuli that bombard him, to arrange the multifarious pushes and pulls into communicable patterns and ideas. With this power to conceptualize and order the flow of life, the self stands outside, transcends, the natural flux.

There is another quality of spirit, one that is not adequately described by rationalism. This is the quintessential "I" that ascends the highest steps in the tower of selfhood and there looks back down upon the reasoning process itself. It is a consciousness aware of consciousness, thus self-consciousness. It is a transcendence that includes not only the capacity to think but to think about oneself in the act of thinking, thus self-transcendence. There is an elusive I that stands out of range of our mightiest efforts to net it. We can never get "in back of" that self which rises above itself in "indefinite regression." Theologians such as Augustine have explored its reaches, laying bare memory and foresight as factors in self-transcendence. Philosophers have lifted up and researched self-determination as a prominent quality of this central selfhood. Mystics have plunged into the depths of personal self-awareness where few have been able to follow, to report the contours of this difficult terrain. But the ordinary man, by thoughtful introspection, can also discern the reality of an I which in its freedom surveys itself—past, present and future—and its world, seeks to affect its destiny and believes it can. Even those who deny the reality of this final dimension of selfhood are forced to presuppose it in their very denial, whenever they use the word I and urge others to accept their determinism.

We have described spirit rather abstractly. However, there is a content and feel associated with it. The higher reaches of selfhood are pervaded by a sense of being related to and claimed by a source and standard outside the self. This awareness expresses itself in a homelessness of the spirit, an inability to locate any meaning worthy of final trust in the world of nature and history. It is informed also with an inchoate perception that what it does is out of accord with what the self most essentially is called to be. And it is furnished also with a dim instinct of what that mandate is, namely, that life can fulfilled only in affirmation of, and harmony with, other lives.

So far our analysis has employed the common currency of secular and philosophical language. But we have reached a point where description of the "facts" available to honest introspection moves on to interpretation and hence to the leap of faith. Niebuhr attributes man's sense of being grasped and judged as having its source in the pressure of an Other on the borders of his awareness. The substance of the mandate which impinges, and the guilt which is generated by the breach of that mandate, is that Other's law of love. The structure through which God makes his presence felt in the conscience of man is the "image of God" in man.

Code Language: The Image of God and our Creatureliness.
While Niebuhr includes reason in the image of God, it is this dalogue in man's subjectivity with another Claimant which more closely defines it. The situation is compared to an eye which has lost its sight but retains its shape and structure. So the self may fail to live out its original purpose of love toward God and man (it has lost the "likeness of God"), but it retains enough of the original design to be aware of what it is made for and restive with what it is not (it still has the "image of God"). Thus the image is that capacity of freedom in man which reflects the freedom of God and is fashioned to fulfill itself in the perfect freedom of self-giving. The freedom is there, aware of its source and end.

Again in contrast to some cultural tendencies, particularly idealist ones, Niebuhr views the self which lives at the confluence of nature and spirit as an unqualified unity. Spirit is not segregated from, or uninfluenced by, the body, as it is in classic and contemporary rationalism. The mind is the body's mind, as in Hebrew thought the soul is the blood's breath. While psychosomatic evidence documents this conviction, it is the biblical belief to which this affirmation is finally

[37]

traced. Pointing also to this unity is the doctrine of the resurrection of the body, to be distinguished from the Greek notion of immortality which viewed the soul as detachable at death from the body. Another biblical thesis about the unity of the self is the doctrine of God as Creator. The God of biblical faith is no divine Mind who orders a neutral or re- calcitrant materiality. Rather, God is both vitality and form, the Author of heaven and earth, things spiritual and material and manifesting this commonality in the creation of a whole man.

As a human being is made in the togetherness of body and spirit, so he is designed for unity within the family of man. We have spoken of the fundamental dependence of the indi- vidual on others for physical survival and growth. Man is fulfilled in spirit as well as nature in and through his com- munal relationships. At the most basic level, his symbol life, his language, is made possible through community. In the higher reaches of his spirit, his self is so designed that it cannot be fulfilled unless it lives in harmony with other selves. That oneness itself is not achievable unless man gives himself for his neighbor. Thus the ground of human life is sociality, and its law is love.

The Dynamics of Man

Anxiety. Life at the juncture just described is not an easy one. Niebuhr finds its most poignant ambiguity in the ultimate yearnings fostered by the image yet frustrated by creaturely moorings. Developing an existentialist motif, shaped particularly by Kierkegaard's analysis of the human predicament, he speaks of an appetite for the infinite whetted by a spirit that is in touch with the transtemporal and made for a goal outside of itself. The spirit, which rises above its natural rootages to view a greater possibility, dis- covers that its expectations stand under the threat of finitude. Man thirsts for the security of the absolute, but

[38]

death seems to render that hope spurious. A pilot trained to fly is mysteriously grounded. The enigma of hobbled flight sets up in man a profound anxiety. He must secure his ego somehow. He must prove that his life is not in vain.

Anxiety is the precondition of sin. It does not force sin into being, for ideally anxiety could be allayed by a serenity derived from a more ultimate security than history can furnish. In fact, anxiety could be transmuted into new levels of creativity. As it works out, anxiety proves to be man's undoing: it is the snake in the Genesis myth, the temptation that is the occasion for man, in his freedom, to choose the fall. The snake in the Genesis story, beguiling Adam and Eve (an account to be taken "seriously, although not literally"), describes the universal tendency of anxious men to look out for number one.

Idolatry. When man chooses himself as the object of first loyalty, he displaces the One who rightly belongs there. Thus the primal sin is idolatry, the wish to be a god. It bends the urge planted in man to give himself in absolute devotion back toward man himself and his programs. The action is described in Genesis as the wish of an incurved self to usurp the prerogatives of Deity. It is the sin of pride, self-elevation, the lethal constant in the life of all men.

This self-regarding impulse lies at the very center of human personality, in the will. Naturalism locates the trouble in man's reason and therefore assumes that a plunge into or alignment with natural vitalities will cure his ailment. Idealism holds that evil lies in either a passion or an ignorance that can be corrected by larger doses of reason. Niebuhr, on the other hand, finds the sickness of man to be in the very freedom which rises above both nature and reason. Since the self is corrupted at its very core, naturalistic and idealistic solutions are exercises in futility. Man's perversity will assert itself in every new configuration arranged by their optimistic proposals. It is a stubborn parasite on human freedom. The enlargement of the very capacity that is singular to man therefore carries with it the threat of destruction as well as the promise of creativity.

Man's egoism displays a particular intransigence at the level of social institutions. Collectivities such as nations and economic systems are especially prone to a destructive self-interest, magnifying the sin that is in the heart of the individual. While Niebuhr summed this thesis up in the title of his early work, *Moral Man and Immoral Society*, in later years he said it should more properly have read, "immoral man and even more immoral society."

Privateering. Self-love takes shapes commensurate with the dimensions of man. Thus sin can express itself in a will to dominate, to lord it over other men. This will to power is related to man's unique stature as spirit, the quality that links him with the Deity and therefore provides him with the occasion to think of himself more highly than he ought to think. This is pride in a derivative sense, an imperialism which forces other men to bow the knee before one's own claims and agendas.

Flight. Self-love can express itself also as a will to powerlessness, as retreat from responsibility into nature's cavernous escape routes. Borrowing and refining the Augustinian category of concupiscence (cleansing it of the notion that it is transmitted by the sex act and limited to "fleshly" sins), Niebuhr speaks of it as a sensuality which seeks to cope with anxiety by flight into forgetfulness and ultimately into self-forgetfulness. It includes the escape into animality, bourgeois mediocrity and the rat race on the one hand, and lassitude or apathy on the other.

The Smoke Screen: Self-righteousness. The self-regarding impulses in man, interlaced as they are with his freedom, regularly hide themselves behind the mask of self-righteousness. Sin is not a simple will to power but a will to power that cloaks itself in virtue. Niebuhr shows the

[40]

similarity between biblical realism about man's "pharisaism" and the concept of ideology in Marx (regnant ideas in class society are the tools of the ruling class) and rationalization in Freud (giving good reasons for real reasons). Each exposes man's feverish effort to veil his imperialism in the garments of the wise and the good. He affirms that the biblical eye sees more deeply than secular realisms, for the latter do not indict themselves for the same pretensions they see in others.

The Destiny of Man

Ranged against man's self-regarding impulses are forces which struggle to contain and redeem them. It is the divine intent that the battle will be waged without ceasing in history, and it is the divine promise that there will be another destiny than the defeat of man.

Counterforce 1: Judgment in History and the Self. Men in their arrogance may defy the law of love, but they cannot defy it absolutely. As the law of life, anything less than mutuality is self-destructive. This lesson is driven home vividly in the conduct of nations and their leaders, as the prophets took pains to point out. Blatant imperialism brings in its wake historical punishment. God acts through this law of mutuality to bring the mighty from their seats. As the essential pattern of life is unity, its violators will pay the price when they tear its fabric. In fact, the consequences of this confrontation can be called the "wrath of God." Niebuhr sometimes describes this recoil of life's essential structure as a "rough justice," for it cannot be detailed with philosophical nicety. There are periods in which the imperious do prosper, and there is no neat punishment commensurate with crime. But over the long haul, the law cannot be breached without disastrous effects.

The counterpart to a large-scale judgment is the out-working of justice in the inner recesses of selfhood about which we have spoken. Inasmuch as the self still carries the marks of its essential mandate to live for others, its self-love is shadowed by guilt. A nagging uneasiness with anything less than self-giving cannot be erased as long as human freedom itself is not aborted. This uneasiness is the fruit of the constant divine impingement on the spirit dimension of selfhood.

Counterforce 2: Healing in History and the Self. In earlier years, and again in much later ones, Niebuhr speaks warmly of the "common grace" turned loose in the world. The arena in which it does its work tends to be on a much smaller scale than that in which judgment manifests itself, such as in the family and in face-to-face relationships. However, it is not altogether absent from the dealings of nations. While the latter prove more fertile soil for chastisement appropriate to the collective evils to which men are so prone, there is also a providence working through the residual moral sense of political entities, a fact that may startle and disprove a too-consistent cynicism about the affairs of nations. This modicum of responsibility may express itself in care for a starving brother nation or a sober restraint on the temptation to exploit a sister's weakness. It is also manifest in the rich elaboration of human potentiality that appears in history, and the cultural and scientific fecundity that moves society. A latter-day appreciation of the Renaissance moved Niebuhr to note these workings, formerly muted.

But it is in the more intimate relations of life that such a grace is more often remarked upon. Thus Niebuhr sees that parental care can provide a sense of security which frees the growing self in turn to love others. He notes as well a conjugal love that both ministers in disaster and liberates the partners to larger meanings. Also, in the forgiveness and compassion of friends and associates, Niebuhr saw a "reflection and refraction" of a more ultimate Mercy. And in the nourishment of the spirit by the past's heritage, and of the body by the intricate network of natural and social relationships, he saw as well the action of a benevolent God.

While Niebuhr had relatively little to say about the world of nature, and often what was said stressed its brutality if not malevolence, there are allusions, particularly in his earlier writings, to its role as a vehicle of grace. Thus he notes that a benevolent natural alchemy, if not overtaxed by man's greedy and/or stupid uses of science technology, will save an urban mass from destruction by its own pollutants. This kind of healing, which can be seen in marvels that run from the body's restorative powers to the recuperation of a tree struck by lightning, is often ignored or missed by a society of cities. Nevertheless it is retained by men who live close to the soil and should be honored by the religious imagination as a sign of a larger good at work.

A Special Work of Hope. An important clue to Niebuhr's understanding of what decisive action God takes to overcome the rebellion of man, and who in fact God is, is found in the use of the analogy of personal relationship. A human being may survey the external shape and behavior of another and grasp something about the nature and character of that second self. But the depth of the other's being is not exposed until the one that is viewed as an *object* becomes a *subject*, uncovering his inner thoughts and shedding light on the meaning of his overt actions. When the other speaks the disclosing word, he draws the first person into a new relationship, out of the role of dispassionate spectator and into that of personal communion.

The processes of historical judgment and grace described above are similar to the external actions of another person. Men experience them, and they can even grasp something of their meaning. Thus God's overt work is described as "general revelation." But the deeper significance of what they confront and dimly perceive is lost upon them until the Self chooses to reveal the inner depths of his heart and mind.

In an obscure slice of Hebrew history the divine Self-disclosure begins. Prophets declare that God has a bone to pick not only with the impious nation but also with the people of the Covenant. History is not simply a contest between the just and the unjust but a struggle in which even the righteous set themselves against the Lord. Within the messianic tradition in Judaism, the prophet looks for the day when a just and merciful God will extirpate evil and reclaim the lost, establishing his Kingdom. But it is never clear how the justice of this God which brooks no evil can be satisfied, and mercy prevail.

The enigma of justice and mercy is resolved in the final disclosure of who God is, in Jesus Christ. The life, teaching and death of Jesus embody the perfect law of love. The pattern of self-giving clarifies the Source of the unity by which the world lives. Jesus' uncalculating love demonstrates the paradox of a self-offering which must animate mutuality if that latter harmony is not to be corrupted by a prudence still caught in the circle of self-interest. But it also dramatizes the fate of heedless care on worldly turf. Perfect love plus sin equals crucifixion.

The cross and its sequel, the resurrection, are transactions that illumine the unsolved problem of the Old Testament and release a power that can cope with the self's own sin. Golgotha reveals a love that absorbs the punishment which an unsentimental justice requires. The God who suffers brings together justice and mercy. In the cross we see a sacrificial love that takes up into itself the punishment which justice demands. The resurrection announces that this self-offering does not end in futility. The happening on a hill corresponds to the deepest level of the structures of reality and its ultimate issue. The Pauline construction of the Galilean story corresponds to Jesus' own understanding of the message of Kingdom of God. He viewed himself as herald and first fruit of the inbreaking waves of a New Commonwealth of peace and righteousness and pointed men ahead to its fulfillment at the end of history.

To return to our analogy of personal relationship, God showed "what was on his mind" in the central events of Jesus. It was a long-suffering love that bore history forward, one whose Word and Act shouldered the consequences of man's rebellion and thereby assured the fulfillment of the divine intention. And as in the human relation, in which loving self-disclosure draws the other into communion, so in this Self-offering, those who have the eyes to see and the ears to hear are driven to penitence and faith. Penitence, because they discover their own implication in mankind's wounding of God. In genuine repentance the self is broken and authentic shattering continues as a lifelong vocation. In and through penitence, faith is born. Faith is the self's trust that its guilt is conquered by a suffering Love.

To faith is added hope. In the rich and murky symbols of the Apocalypse there comes the promise that the incompleteness and ambiguities of self and society will be overcome at "the end of history." The Christian doctrine of the End conceives the fulfillment of the biblical hope as a transfiguration different from anything possible "in history." It thus avoids the illusions of those who claim too much for their own achievements or plans. As the vision is "out ahead," and thus in some relationship with our own life on earth, it also calls into question notions of fulfillment which dismiss the significance of this life and work for an escape into an eternity "above history." The symbol of Last Things, stripped of literalistic talk about the furniture of heaven and the temperature of hell, affirms the continuity with, and importance of, the historical pilgrimage and our efforts in it. It also dignifies our individuality and assures the solidity of its rootage in a final reality which is not identifiable with our manageable and conventional visibilities.

To hope is added love. And for a man who is remembered by many as one of the world's most searching moralists, we devote a full section to this third theological virtue.

The Works of Love

The Test: Social Relevance. The issue of faith and hope is love. It was the works of love, their meaning and application, that formed the center of gravity of Niebuhr's thought. Early in his Detroit pastorate he remarked that the ministry was taking on a new luster as he gave more attention to its ethical concerns and less to its metaphysical quandaries. That commitment to the use of the Christian faith as a resource to illumine the issues of war and peace, international relations, poverty, economic justice, race and sex persisted and grew stronger as his career unfolded. Niebuhr summed up his way of doing theology in the observation that it is only natural for a professor of social ethics to use as a definitive test, "By their fruits ye shall know them."

Niebuhr's absorption in the righting of social wrongs expressed itself in a moral pragmatism. That is, he evaluated concepts, secular or churchly, in terms of their capacity to shed light upon, or provide incentive for, the solution of human problems. A favorite two-pronged test was the ability of an idea to avoid the "Scylla" of fanaticism or the "Charybdis" of despair. The former, a distortion of man's freedom, represents the self-righteous fury which sooner or later brings chaos to men and nations. The latter, a perversion of man's ties to nature, often the result of a shattered megalomania, is a flight from moral responsibility. Variations on these two poles include sentimentality, self-righteousness and complacency on the one hand, and mediocrity, lassitude and sensuality on the other. Thus the question of how best to execute the ethical test became the forum in which his "apologetic" dialogue was carried out. It was the standard to which he had recourse in comparing the validity of biblical themes with other claimants to truth.

However, it should be added that while the moral test can invalidate an idea that could not produce fruits, and lend credence to ones that could, it was not offered simplistically as the method of final accreditation of the truth of the Christian faith. A good moral record assures a thesis of candidacy. But Christian faith, as a personal commitment, cannot be generated by moral argumentation. The birth of genuine conviction comes by way of penitence and faith.

Perfectionism and its Problems. As Niebuhr's earliest wrestling with the major questions of a love ethic came in his struggle with pacifism, we root our exploration there. The religious pacifist read the rigorous New Testament admonitions to turn the cheek and go the second mile as literal counsels of nonviolence in personal conduct and public affairs. A frequent corrolary was the assumption that this behavior meshed with the deepest structures of human life. Self-abnegation would be reciprocated in kind, and social problems would find their solution by obedience to the Sermon on the Mount. Thus an essential goodness in each man, a spark of divinity, would be fanned into a blaze of goodwill by the action of those who practice the ethics of sacrificial love.

Niebuhr honored the pacifist testimony to selflessness, for he saw it as pointing to the pinnacle of the Christian ethic embodied in the life of Christ and, beyond that, in the suffering love of God himself. Anything less than self-giving did indeed inject poison into the world's bloodstream. Further, he believed that the small enclaves of pacifist witness, particularly those with religious roots, such as the Mennonites, did serve as the reminder of the heights of Christian expectation and as a judgment of conscience on man's violence and self-aggrandizement.

One ingredient, however, was missing in the pacifist calculus: human sin. The absence of that factor skewed the pacifists' analysis of behavior and accounted for the futility of their program of social change. Man's self-regarding impulses made their impact felt in several ways. For one, in the enemy who was to be won by actions of perfect love. Given his will to power and exploitative instinct, he would be prone to interpret the gesture of nonviolence as weakness, rather than be humbled by its kindnesses. The results would then be not only the crucifixion of the nonviolent, which an authentic pacifist is fully ready to accept, but also the sacrifice of those innocents and values which might otherwise have been protected, if less pacific means had been resorted to. The magnifying of the exploitative instinct in large collectivities rendered the pacifist counsel even more dangerous as a political guideline. The Nazi phenomenon was a dramatic case in point. Not only the annihilation of the Jew but the crumbling of the Western charter of freedom and justice would result from the totalitarian juggernaut, if the way of nonviolence were to be chosen.

The rejection of an ideological pacifism did not preclude, however, a pragmatic one. Niebuhr believed that in dealing with the relatively civilized British conscience, a Gandhi could effect change by passive resistance. And in the 1960's Niebuhr acknowledged the effectiveness of Martin Luther King, Jr.'s tactics in a conscience-stricken America exposed, as well, to world opinion. However, he consistently underscored the naïveté of a doctrinaire pacifism which based its strategies on the fundamental goodness of man.

Niebuhr saw yet another illusion of pacifism to be the failure to probe its own motives and conduct. He sometimes wondered out loud about the bitterness of the attack of pacifists on those who took issue with their position. The impossibility of the ideal was demonstrated by the very ones who so loudly espoused it.

The Relevance of an Impossible Ideal. If the absolute love ethic could not be applied directly to human affairs, then what use was it? Niebuhr cited at least five ways in which it was relevant as an "impossible possibility" (a term later abandoned because it lent itself too easily to misunderstanding), some of which we have already alluded to in Niebuhr's affirmation of the pacifist role:

1. It is testimony to the fundamental structure of the universe, the law of love. Whoever saves his life will lose it. Self-concern has the seeds of destruction in it.

2. The love absolute represents a lure toward higher approximations of neighborly concern and a judge upon lower ones. Man cannot rest easily in any setting less than that in which there is a self-giving harmony of life with life.

3. It is witness to the paradox that the spirit of selflessness

is the only condition upon which mutuality itself can thrive. The give-and-take that harmony requires cannot be launched or sustained by prudence, for that kind of calculation is itself caught in the trap of self-interest and will tend to poison human relationships.

4. Because there are residual traces of grace and goodness in human self and society, there are some points of contact for self-giving love. This is particularly true of the more intimate human relationships. They can trigger response in kind. Sacrificial care can move others to penitence and reciprocating kindness. Thus there are some tangents in history to what is, in the last analysis, a transhistorical standard.

5. Perfect sacrificial love, eminently displayed in the life and death of Jesus, is the only rock on which the obtuseness of man can finally be shattered. Here the dim perception that the self is made for selflessness is clarified. Before the cross the penitence is born that calls into question the imperious self, and faith in the divine forgiveness is nourished.

Reachable Norms. While a love absolutism serves these purposes, it cannot provide viable guidelines for day-to-day ethics, especially social ethics. For this we must scale down love to derivative norms that presuppose the self-regarding factors on the human scene; we must translate absolute love into more realizable actions.

Mutual love is such a first de-escalation. It is kindred to sacrificial love in that it wills the harmony of life with life. The difference is that the former is based on considerations of prudence, rather than the latter's spontaneity and uncalculating self-giving. The self affirms the interest of other selves because the result is a society in which the self's own interest can best be served. The limits of this ethic were cited earlier. Also, mutuality is a goal that can be moved toward only at the pace of manifest self-interest. In any case it does serve as a social directive that comes within the range of historical possibility.

A notch below the level of mutual love is equal justice. Its link with the New Testament absolute is that it echoes the "as thyself" of the love injunction. By this standard we are advised to be ready to give to each man as much as we claim for ourselves. Justice of any kind presupposes the conflict of life with life and seeks to sort out conflicting claims. Each man deserves his due. In the case of equal justice, equity is that due.

Other principles that implement the more absolute standard in the context of the society of sinful men are freedom and order. As these apply more directly to the political arena, we shall treat them there. Thus having made our way from theological premise through the law of love to questions of application in the city of man, it is only natural to turn now to the latter's moil and toil.

III
Political Shoots

The title of Niebuhr's book, *Faith and Politics* (1968), points to the rhythm we are tracing. His theology and ethics flow naturally toward political reflection and action of two kinds: confrontation with epochal cultural currents and shrewd commentary on, and participation in, the events of the day.

Measuring History's Movements

The major political options of the century pass in review, as do their premises about man and history. Let us sample a few of the analyses.

Marxism. Niebuhr moved from an appreciative yet critical opinion of Marxism (in the Depression he accepted the label of "Christian Marxist") to a view in which his disagreements and hostility far outweighed the things that he could acknowledge as corrective of capitalist injustices. However, there are recurring motifs in his evaluation which we shall identify, indicating emphases that grow or diminish.

The capitalism that threw off the yoke of medieval aristocracy knew about the corruptability of political power. But freedom from the feudal lord did not produce a just society. The invisible hand of Adam Smith and the presumed laws of the free market that were to produce human welfare did not materialize. Instead the new bourgeoisie amassed an economic power that caused untold harm. Marx, moved by a passionate humanism, surveyed the effects of a nineteenth-century laissez-faire capitalism that brought dehumanization and death to countless workers, and labeled private property as the virus in the system. Niebuhr believed that Marx was correct in pinpointing the economic failures as a source of the era's miseries (although wrong in failing to probe below the profit motive to a more basic level of culpability). The control of human life by an economic elite and its machinery had to be challenged and checked. Until 1948 this meant, for Niebuhr and his associates in the Fellowship of Christian Socialists, the common ownership of the natural resources and the basic means of production. However, it became increasingly clear that the Marxist program of extirpating evil by removing private property produced a new agglomeration of power which promptly went to the head of its holders. A Marxist society, blinded by its anthropological illusions, was unable to deal with this new oligarchy and its tyrannies. A similar naïvete plagued democratic socialism, resulting in its failure to provide for incentives and for protection against the exploitation of a persisting self-interest.

Niebuhr moved to a less doctrinaire posture in dealing with the abuses of economic power. The Christian Marxist of the thirties became the Christian pragmatist of the fifties and beyond. Political power was stressed as a check to inordinate economic power. Property itself, always bearing in it the seeds of injustice when growing inordinate, was seen in a limited way as a method of securing society against the development of political, social or other economic monoliths. The new pragmatism meant most of all that no ideology could be a reliable guide for solving the complex problems of a technological society. Each situation had to be judged on its own merits, with an eye always kept open for the corrupting tendencies of ascending power. Efforts had to be exerted to build balancing structures in the social fabric.

Niebuhr credited Marxism with a deeper perception of man's egoism than most secular competitors. In several ways: in its "catastrophism," it saw that those who control society could not be persuaded out of their bastions by reason or preachment. And in its concept of ideology, it exposed the taint of self-interest in professedly objective structures of law, politics, morality and religion. Because of its explanation of these tendencies in terms of private property, Marxism failed to allow for the persistence of this taint in its own programs and dreams. Thus it fell prey to the mystical glorification of classless society which the facts did not warrant. And it succumbed to a utopianism that either clung fanatically to its delusions, on the one hand, or was driven to despair by the shattering of its dreams, on the other. The era of Stalinist and Russian imperialism were the fruits of the utopian fanaticism, and the ex-Marxist dropouts from the social struggle were the children of disillusionment.

While Niebuhr's assessment of Marxism was couched in economic and political terms, he sought to push below these to its fundamental premises about man and his destiny. In fact, he sought to show that both its strengths and weaknesses are traceable more directly to its existence as a "religion" than as an alleged scientific account of social processes. Its passion for justice and dream of a world in which each gives unselfishly, and has his needs satisfied by society, is linked to the Judeo-Christian tradition. Interlaced with this prophetic note is an interpretation of history which locates its origin in a paradisical primitive communism from which men fell away by the poison of private property. But the gods of history will not rest easy with this fall, so the story goes. A mysterious dialectical providence moves by the motors of economic need through succeeding societies to a final denouement in which class polarities come to a head in the Armageddon struggle of late capitalism. At this time, those born to redeem history, the proletariat, are raised up to deliver the final blow to the dragon in a violent paroxysm, whose issue will be a world at one with itself. So reads the creed in the *Manifesto* that Engels described originally as a "catechism."

Liberalism. As Niebuhr could find no solutions for twentieth-century man in fundamental Marxism, he rejected also "liberalism," the other political and social creed that claimed the allegiance of countless contemporaries and informed much of the style of his own country, particularly its intellectual leadership.

Taking its rise in Renaissance and Enlightenment understandings of man, the liberal social philosophy believed in the essential goodness of human nature. Trusting especially in the reasonableness of man, it saw no recalcitrance which could not be eliminated. Impediments to progress there were: ignorance, the passions of an animal nature whose residues still clung on, outworn social institutions. But education and moral suasion were tools of change that could overcome these obstacles.

In fact, they were going about their business doing just that. The obsolete social forms and irrationalities of the past were being progressively sloughed off in man's ascent. History was a satisfying pilgrimage. It showed clear signs of advance and held out the promise of an upward escalator trip. The evolution manifest in nature was also at work on the human plane, moving the race into successively greater degrees of goodwill and harmony.

These sanguine assumptions and expectancies were characteristic of all exponents of the liberal creed, including the pragmatist in the John Dewey tradition and the Social Gospel reformer. The premises were married to several other ideas which marked the mainstream movement as bourgeois, although they did not characterize the left end of the spectrum such as the socialist fringe. One of these was an individualism which believed that the dignity of a person was best upheld by freeing him from the restraints of the community. Indeed, man chooses to work for his own self-interest, but the result of that impulse would be arranged by benevolent natural processes—crafted by an Invisible Hand—so that the egoism of each would work to the well-being of all. Individualism was bourgeois in that it furnished the rising middle classes with a battle cry against feudal restraints which slowed the engines of commercial and industrial development.

[54]

With its suspicion of the communal motif, the individualist spirit of bourgeois liberalism had little time for talk about the social matrix of selfhood. Self-made man pulled himself up by his own bootstraps. Those who fell by the wayside were moral dropouts, to be scorned—or, at best, pitied. Society and its structures neither broke men nor saved them. Each individual by the rugged strength of his will and hard work had to make his own way.

Niebuhr characteristically sketched in broad brush strokes the qualities of the liberal creed and then, in equally sweeping but penetrating judgments, lined out an indictment. Liberalism, especially its bourgeois mainstream, was refuted by history itself. It was unprepared for the horrendous sequel to its ascendency. Thus the harmless self-interest it assumed would do its benevolent work turned into a holocaust of starvation, exploitation and depression for countless millions. And on the heels of that came total government, total wars and programs of genocide which sent reeling the sanguine forecasts of a culture which had assumed that barbarity had been long left behind with the primitives. The contours of its own institutions began to show through the tattered garments of modern society, demonstrating that man was much more a creature of his social environment than its individualism assumed, making and breaking him by its machinery.

Historical evidence should make it clear, affirmed Niebuhr, that faith in man's goodness and reason is misplaced. Man's problem is more than a lack of social intelligence or cultural lag. The trouble lies at the very center of his being, a corrupt will. Therefore, every advance in history in which man's ingenuity spawns technological growth or social reorganization is not an unambiguous step forward. Along with the creativity, which the liberal spirit did unshackle and discern to be limitless, goes the risk of continued and even more devastating forms of destruction. History supplies no evidence that good triumphs over evil.

The miscalculations of individualism must also be corrected by a more organic understanding of man. He is not an isolated atom of pure will. He is a creature of nature and the social network which supports and can destroy him.

As with Marxism, so with liberalism; Niebuhr found strengths as well as weaknesses. While rejecting its unwarranted optimism about man, he denied as well notions of man's total depravity and complete cynicism about our social future. Thus he affirmed in a modest and qualified way the human potential which liberalism celebrated, albeit too noisily and uncritically. The openness to the future, the readiness to call into question the intellectual or institutional status quo, the pursuit of free inquiry, the open debate in the marketplace of ideas—all these characteristics of the liberal spirit he believed to be commitments whose loss would be perilous to society.

Key Elements in Critique and Construction

The Real. The error common to both Marxism and liberalism is the failure to detect the depth and persistence of man's self-regarding impulses, especially as they mold his collectivities. An alternate perspective will have at its center a realistic estimate of human nature, its perversities, and the inclination to obscure them. Realism will be alert to any accumulation of power, wary of its temptations, suspicious of its protestations of interest in the common welfare, committed to the dispersing and democratizing of power, surrounding it with checks and balances.

Because of the disruptive inclinations of human sin, realism will also struggle for the measure of social order that makes human association livable. While checking and equilibrating power is a necessary step toward tolerable justice, that effort assumes a fabric of human community made possible only by the political restaint and ordering of egoism, hence the necessity for "order" as a social goal. But realism will also point to that kind of order in which the restraints of government are imposed by the citizenry itself.

[56]

Liberty is the protection of the people against the tyranny of political power. It is also the context in which the full resources of the community can be uncovered and harnessed for the public weal.

Thus, realism points to the principles of equal power, a just distribution of society's resources and opportunities, an order that guarantees the social fabric will not be torn by conflicting interests, and a freedom to control that order and release its human potential.

The Ideal. While Niebuhr stresses the realistic factors because of the high visibility of overoptimistic estimates of man and and his social designs, there is another political lodestar also at work. The pull of the ideal, as well as the push of the real, is a factor in Niebuhr's orientation. While the law of love in its perfectionist form cannot be exported neatly from heaven to earth, it does its work from "out ahead," illumining the path that is to be traversed and luring to a fuller approximation of its harmonies. Thus love declares for the dignity of each human being and pleads for the designing of a society in which the fulfillment of each life is the goal. A Christian love, tutored in the sinfulness of the terrain on which it must operate, strives for equal justice noting the "as thyself" in the neighbor-love mandate. Another "due" which reflects the dignity accorded each self by love, and honors the unique capacity of transcendence associated with that dignity, is political freedom. And there must be a mechanism to insure the implementation of justice and freedom derived from love. Thus the function of government is not only the negative restraint of evil but also the positive guaranteeing of the fruits of the society to all its participants.

Thus *both* the real and the ideal provide the makings of Niebuhr's political philosophy, the former much more explicitly so than the latter, thus warranting the description of Neibuhr's position as "Christian realism." But it should be noted that both from "below" and "above," i.e., from the past experience of man's recalcitrance and from the future

Goal of his pilgrimage, are to be heard the call for justice, equality, freedom and order. Fundamental premises about man and derivative moral mandates are at work in his more general reflections on domestic and international affairs. We turn next to them.

The Nation

When we focus on the mature thought of Niebuhr, we move from a variety of Christian socialism to a Christian pragmatism. That is, although guided by the postulates cited above, there is no attempt to stamp out a blueprint for the social order. Niebuhr's method is inductive. He begins with the situation and tests it for adequacy, rather than imposing a deductive scheme upon it. He views the political scene in experimental terms, hoping to learn from the mistakes of a venture launched, accommodating to new realities, spurred by new insights. His almost British "muddling through" approach is related to his conviction that while history is not simply an organism, neither is it an artifact easily contrived by human ingenuity. One therefore works with the givens, molding them experimentally in the double light of the real and the ideal.

The Struggle for Justice. Following this task of beginning with the givens, Niebuhr takes off from the liberal West in which he finds himself. With a characteristic running start in history, he notes the struggles of the nineteenth-century with dehumanizing industrial baronies. This arrogance of economic power produced a countervailing thrust in the labor movement. The trade unions demonstrated that the assumptions of a self-regulating capitalism were fictitious. The worker had to organize to protect himself against the exploitative tendencies of a *laissez-faire* economy and its power wielders. Moreover, he discovered that his fight for basic social security required the assistance of government.

Thus political power became a weapon in the struggle to check economic power and redress its wrongs. While an earlier and ideological Niebuhr scorned the New Deal as a palliative, he later came to view the Roosevelt era as a laboratory in which many of the inequalities of early capitalism were corrected by social-welfare pragmatism.

On the heels of the worker came the human rights fight of the black citizen. Long grieved by the "American dilemma" of a high charter of freedom and equality yet a flagrant abuse of it in the treatment of the Negro, Niebuhr saw the freedom movement, particularly under the leadership of Martin Luther King, Jr., as making wise use of social and political power to redress old grievances and to give a new sense of dignity to the oppressed. As in the case of the blue collar worker, so also with the black citizen; not only was elementary justice to be accorded to all the citizenry in these upsurges, but the freedom movement was releasing long-untapped resources among black citizens that would ultimately benefit the whole community.

While government served as a balance wheel to other centers of tempted power, and as an instrument of distributive justice, it was itself a power that had to be watched and moderated both from within and without. From within, the wisdom of the founding fathers had provided a system of checks and balances—legislative, judicial and executive. From without, the pluralism of the institutions and interests of a democratic society helped to restrain monolithic tendencies, as did the election system itself.

The Welfare State. As Niebuhr viewed the development of the democratic state in the West, he saw Judeo-Christian and Renaissance values combine with the exigencies and dynamics of a technopolitan society and, with an increasingly empirical and pragmatic temper, follow a tortuous route of trial and error until it produced the modern "welfare state." He did not believe this vast social experiment was neatly exportable to other societies at different stages of growth, nor did he claim eternal validity for it. But for the conditions of a highly developed technological West it seemed to provide a tolerable mix of the best elements of the two competing creeds—planning and freedom—which in their extreme Marxist and bourgeois liberal form had proved inadequate. This mix, which guaranteed maneuvering room for its citizens within an order that acknowledged its responsibility to provide for the basic needs of all (although yet unable to match promise with performance, especially for the poor and the black), succeeded by its cultivation of a variety of centers of power and by a charter with commitments to the well-being of all. Its modest realism about how justice can be secured, and its modest idealism about the possibilities of achieving it, reflected the human condition itself. That estate suggests the viability of this kind of social arrangement. As Niebuhr put it in one of his memorable epigrams: "Man's capacity for justice makes democracy possible; but man's inclination to injustice makes democracy necessary."[1]

International Affairs

As Marxism and bourgeous liberalism, planning and freedom, provided the foci for Niebuhr's political thought in other areas, so in the sphere of world affairs the giant embodiments of these polarities, the Soviet Union and the United States, occupied the center of his reflection. This is especially true in the years in which Niebuhr exercised a significant influence among political scientists and those in government circles. Both Russia and America live by social myths. Under the battlements of each huddle numerous client nations, as the medieval castle hovered protectively over its constituent lands and towns.

Russia. Marxism made its first significant conquest in Russia. While rejected in the European technical society for which it was ideologically designed, it took root in a pastoral culture whose postwar deterioration made it ripe for the ardent revolutionary schemes of Lenin. Using formulas whose reference points were the decadence of late capitalism, Russian communism hauled a peasant society doggedly into a twentieth-century technological setting with a totalitarian grip. The price of that pull was the horrendous brutalities of the Stalinist era and the elimination of the step of political democracy, through which Europe and the West had painfully passed and found to be the prerequisite of a just society. While the Soviet Union successfully negotiated its way into an advanced technology, one which boasted some stunning victories over the less tightly run Western democracies, its life was now in the hands of a political elite vulnerable to the same temptations of power to which the rejected economic oligarchs had fallen prey. As Marxism mistakenly located evil in property as such, it failed to build into its system protection against the corruption that can affix itself to any structure of power.

The aggrandizing impulse meshed with national self-esteem to generate an imperialism which hid itself under a righteous ideology. Purporting to be the evangelist of a communism out to save the world from bourgeois mendacity, the Soviet Union extended the borders of its influence wherever capitalistic expansion displayed its Achilles heel or a moribund colonialism beat its undignified retreat. And if any of those gathered under its wing stepped out of line, a Hungary or a Czechoslovakia, that would be too bad. What was originally a more pugnacious imperialism, however, mellowed somewhat as Russia's economy provided more creature comforts to its citizens. Now the old Marxist cry that the proletariat had nothing to lose but its chains sounded a little hollow. Also, the terror of a nuclear war had its sobering effect on the Kremlin. Expansionist propensities took more the turn of aid to developing nations, very similar to the technical assistance of the West, along with support of a more military nature. And here and there agreements were reached to moderate a too calamitous confrontation with the West.

As Russia flirted with coexistence, Niebuhr saw a new China rising to claim the title of champion of the world proletariat, declaring Russia a revisionist heretic. Much further from the security reached by the Soviet Union, it was far less ready for accommodation with the West and more explosive in its rhetoric. Also as a nation of color in the way Russia was not, it laid claim to the title of chief antagonist of the wealthy white oppressor. As with Russia, so with China; the ideology, heightened even further by claims to righteous purity, served to hide national ambitions that were beginning to manifest themselves around its borders and beyond.

The United States. Against the Bear and the Tiger, the Eagle saw itself as the protector of herds of weaker game. America, cradled in liberty, driven by a Wilsonian vision of universal self-determination, would protect the old stag and the young fawn from the terrors of the forest. Niebuhr believed that there was enough truth in this myth to include as a plank in U.S. foreign policy the readiness to place limits on the expansionist zeal of Communist nations, especially Russia, which had the technical ability to implement its rhetoric. Of particular importance was it to guard the European laboratory of social democracy.

American idealism was compounded with its own brand of imperial ambition. It was manifest in the too-eager desire to impose its democratic traditions, developed in an unusually hospitable environment, on nascent countries not similarly equipped and under a more rapid technological survival time schedule. It could be seen as well in a neocolonial economic expansionism in developing countries. Add to this a major miscalculation and some accidents of history, and one gets the anguish of Vietnam. Drawn into a civil war by our ideology of self-determination and the need for naval bases in Asia, America's military prestige became tarnished by the tenacity of effective guerrilla forces. Meanwhile its moral prestige was also soiled by a heavy-handed employment of the new technology of devastation and its reliance upon a suspect military coterie. In our persistence in the war Niebuhr believed we were encouraging the move we most fear, a drawing closer of the enemy to China and to the orthodox Marxism our policy of this period alleged to contain.

While America has arrived at a workable welfare-state democracy for its own technologically advanced society, Niebuhr believed that it should not impose this formula in contexts which did not have similar conditions. Thus America had the advantage of a common language, ethnic communities that either melted into the mainstream or learned to live with one another, or common cultural commitments. In the new nations of other continents, these problems had not yet been worked out, and the give-and-take of the political forum had not yet been worked through. Therefore it is possible that one-party governments, as in Tunisia, must be considered options immediately available, and better than doctrinaire totalitarianism which could wreak greater havoc.

While the giants stagger about in their awkward moves, a Third World is born and grows. Associating the West with the colonial foot it is prying loose from its neck, beguiled by the utopian ideology, impressed by the industrial accomplishments of Russia, the new nations gravitate toward the Marxist option, although not necessarily into the Communist camp. Niebuhr pressed the West to its responsibility for massive development aid so that these new countries could generate their own political forms and style free of old imperialisms of the right or left.

The British Way. But the same ambiguity that is to be found in all human constructs he saw as well in imperialism. Niebuhr lifted up an oft-forgotten creative dimension, citing the tutorial role of Great Britain as it disengaged from its colonialism and took part in the new entity, the Commonwealth. Thus an old imperialism as it liquidates its heritage plants the seeds for a new civil order. Of course, even this was not without decidedly mixed motives; Britain saw the trade possibilities and other supports which would derive from this option. For all that, Niebuhr always esteemed the British way, both in its pragmatic evolution of justice in internal affairs and its openness to change in external dealings with other nations. This esteem was symbolized by his acknowledgment of Churchill as the greatest statesman of the century, for all the latter's sentimental attachment to the days of British hegemony manifest in his reluctance to end the British rule in India.

Unless the stalemate of nuclear horror fails and triggers the suicide of the race, the maneuvers and counter-maneuvers of the major powers are destined to be with us for years and perhaps centuries to come. They will be adjudicated, Niebuhr believed, at least in the foreseeable future, not by a utopian world government for which there is as yet no social organism to give it body, but by a wise statecraft. That statecraft will be moved both by the ideal of a tolerable mutuality and by a realism which takes into account collective egoisms and the attendant righteous pretensions of all the contenders for world power.

IV

Realism and Vision

A new breed of visionary is coming center stage. The political revolutionary dreams of a better world that drives him to call into question all that is, in the light of what might be. The neomystic experiments with an expanded consciousness which purports to see through and beyond the drab and dreary commonplaces. The futurist spins out scenarios of the year 2000. Whatever form it takes, vision begins to nudge our absorption in the "now" and its visibilities. The "not yet" and the "can't-be-seen" exercise a new attraction.

Criticism of Niebuhr and his sober reminders of life's limitations comes, predictably, from the visionaries. "Realism makes people afraid to walk on water!" declares an innovative spirit. Critics assert that realism is so preoccupied with balancing power blocks and practicing the art of the possible that commitment to the radical social change necessary for our times is never generated. It lacks a passion for openness to the future, for doing the undoable, thinking the unthinkable, seeing the unseen. Now is the time for mind-blowing, future orientation, revolutionary hope, not captivity to empirical givens, mesmerism with the ambiguities of the present, compromising reformism. It is the age of dreaming of life's possibilities, not sober realism about its impossibilities.

Those dubious about realism point to the political timidity of some self-declared "Niebuhrians." Critics are also quick to note that prominent disciples of Niebuhr have little good to say about the New Left, political or ecclesiastical, nor are they often found in the front ranks of war protest and resistance. Further, the resources for Christian-Marxist dialogue in Niebuhrian thought seem to be used more as ammunition for attack than as data for pursuing a common inquiry. In short, visionaries, through their observation of realists and their reading of Niebuhr himself, tend to find Christian realism to be a brake rather than a motor of political and religious forward movement in our era.

As I have been caught up in the currents of a theology of hope, and believe that the visionary's time has come in both the political and religious communities, my own struggle has been to integrate convictions about man's ambiguity with those that affirm a hopeful futurity. Out of this painful pilgrimage, I have come to believe that vision and realism can travel together and, in fact, desperately need each other. Our task in this chapter, therefore, will be to explore the promise of Niebuhrian realism for an age of Aquarians.

The Hidden Vision in Niebuhr

The first thing that must be done is to expose the misrepresentations of Niebuhr's own position, distortions traceable often to self-proclaimed realists. Christian realism in Niebuhrian idiom is neither cynicism of the spirit nor political Machiavellianism. There *is* a vision of the Kingdom of God which is the lure and judge of all human attitudes and acts. This precludes opportunism, accommodation to the status quo, or conscienceless compromise. To practice the art of the politically possible does not erase the dream out ahead, a dream that constantly exerts its pull toward more imaginative goals and leaves one impatient with, and penitent about, its fragmentary embodiments. And in that history short of the Kingdom's coming, there are what Niebuhr calls "indeterminate possibilities" for man. Such limitless achievement is thinkable because the image of God in man, though defaced, has not been obliterated. And futher, the Kingdom itself is at work in our midst as foretaste and earnest, though not as finale. There is also in Niebuhr a confidence in the ultimate completion of the incomplete, expressed in the myth of the "end of history," a belief that fortifies the activist against the despairs as well as the illusions of those who "have hope only in this life."

Vision Bashful, Realism Bold

These affirmations are buried down deep in the Niebuhrian literature. They are less visible in the widely read political commentary than in the sermonic and theological material. One has to dig hard for them, too, because of the overlay of popular interpretations which mine only the surface ore of his frequent reflection on history's ambiguities and corruptions. It is also true that Niebuhr, in his period of greatest prominence, accented the negative in Christian realism. And indeed it would seem obscene to talk about visions when nightmares were a reality in Belsen, Dachau and Auschwitz, and when the shattering of dreams was a daily occurrence in an era of depression, totalitarianism, unchallenged racism and global war. In such times, the custodian of Christian realism, the church, not only continued, in the main, to prattle about the goodness of man and his upward progress but relied on programs of moral preachment or personal conversion to change demonic social structures, and failed to see the evil that veiled itself in self-righteousness. Could a prophet talk of an aborning "shalom" in that era? The false ones did indeed cry "peace" when there wasn't any. The harsh accents of a frowning Niebuhr, indicting utopianism, naïveté, and the pretentious visionary, had to be the right sounds for that time of trouble and self-deception.

Vision Bold, Realism Bashful

What is to the foreground in one act of the human drama

may not be necessarily so in the next. In an era of rising expectation and determination from those long submerged—the poor, the black, the woman, the new nation, the consumer, the young—a new momentum forward asserts itself. In a time when an accelerating science-technology holds out the promise of making real the age-old dreams of feeding the hungry, giving sight to the blind and hearing to the deaf, enabling the lame to walk and even raising the dead, new hopes appear on the horizon. Put these developments together with the growing realization that hopelessness is a self-fulfilling prophecy, that future-orientation is needed to anticipate the horrendous evil that might descend upon an otherwise drifting, goalless society, that radical openness to change befits radically changing circumstances, and you get celebration of history's possibilities and the emergence of the visionary. It is significant that Martin Luther King, Jr., who declared to the end of his life that Reinhold Niebuhr was one of the major influences on his thought, and who knew personally more than most men the evil of which the world is capable, will be remembered as the one who taught a generation to say, "I have a dream," and to act on it.

While realism will mute its trumpets in an era of hope, it will not, it must not, be tuned out. As John Bennett put it in an important symposium on this issue, "Nothing has happened to refute the realistic analysis of the stubbornness of evil in society or the tragic side of history. No return to a pre-Niebuhrian optimism is possible."[1] Not only is this impossible for Christian realists, but it is equally impossible for those who think of themselves as Christian hopers. For them too the Dream is always out ahead, goading us to reach for it, driving us to set up signs in our history toward it, but ever eluding our grasp.

At what points, then, is the reminder of the "stubbornness of evil" a crucial component in a theology of hope and politics of the future?

Contesting Entrenched Power

It is interesting to note that one of Niebuhr's most persistent theological New Left critics, Richard Shaull, bases his call
for an antiestablishment coalition on the thesis that levers of
power are needed to shake up the status quo. That is cer-
tainly a Niebuhrian observation. Corrupt and obsolete institutions are not changed by moral suasion but by counter-
pressures, economic, social and political. This insight has
played an important role in some of the current struggles of
the dispossessed and forgotten. The human rights revolution
has assumed the necessity of organizing the black community
to wrest its freedom from autocracies and paternalisms. The
movement has no illusions about the effectiveness of reason
and conscience alone to do the job. Thus in this era of revolt
against old oligarchies, the Niebuhrian wisdom about the
stubbornness of entrenched power, its pretensions to virtue
and the need to muster countervailing pressures is as fresh as
ever. Niebuhr, in his period of greatest influence, applied it to
the confrontation of the worker with industrial baronies and
to the battle against totalitarianism. Current struggles are in
many respects equivalents.

We can anticipate that the succeeding decades of this
century will bring with them the need of new waves of the
dehumanized to organize for their rights. Will that include
the aged? The completing of the revolution of women? Perhaps even the struggle of the "humanoid"? Who knows what
the next colony of oppressed people will be. As long as man
remains man, with the freedom to control his life, society
must protect itself from monolithic decision-making by the
dispersion of its power, and "the weak things of the world
and the despised" press their case through corporate instruments of strength. It is by such means, in this sinful world,
that God "has put down the mighty from their thrones, and
exalted those of low degree."

As the submerged need the realistic Niebuhrian analysis in
the human community at large, so too, in the smaller circle

of church life, the lessons of power will have to be learned. The appropriation of such wisdom will not come quickly in the church's own household, even by those ready to apply it in the secular struggles. "No politics in the church" and the hopes for building a model of loving community in Christ's own covenant community have long been unchallenged premises. Yet, paradoxically, it may mean that the church's own visionaries have to develop organs of power within the Body of Christ itself if their own vision is to be kept alive.

The visionaries nourished by the dreams of King, Pope John and Dietrich Bonhoeffer have found themselves increasingly under attack by a religious establishment reluctant to follow the calls to servanthood and updating. While this has resulted in a significant exodus of disillusioned dreamers, weary of contending with entrenched ecclesiastical interests, it has also brought into being vehicles of countervailing power created to challenge a complacent institution. Sometimes they take the form of the caucus, the power base, even the party within denominations, congregations and the ecumenical movement, to press their cause, elect their candidates and provide a supportive community, psychological as well as political, for their constituents. At other times they appear as "parastructures" which operate outside the orbit of conventional church life—the "underground church," a "new form" of mission in a community such as a coffeehouse or renewal center, a revival of the concept of a religious order on a local or national basis—whose presence and style call into question the business-as-usual church activity, draining off the restless from the latter and thus threatening a serious loss of creativity, energy and even money.

One significant development of this type, related to the "crunch in the churches" between traditionalists and renewers, is the birth and growth of the clergy union. With the increasing dropout rate of renewal-oriented pastors, efforts are being made to organize support systems for those who face the sanctions of either an intransigent hierarchy or an autocratic congregation. Thus visionary churchmen, clergy and lay, organize and must continue to do so within or along-side the institution, borrowing the learnings of an era of realism to carry out their own hopes.

Temptations of Ascending Power

Those within the Christian community who are associated with the humanizing forces, and who provide some ideo-logical cover for them, sometimes question the wisdom of talk about "confession of sin" to their compatriots. And they have particular trouble with the Niebuhrian concern to expose the pride and mixed motives of the committed. Thus it is declared that it is not "privateering" which should pre-occupy us, for a healthy surge forward may in fact be hobbled by too much talk of its ambiguities and pretensions. Rather, it is "sloth" which should trouble us, the retreat from the barricades. In any case, the revolution of the minor-ities of today is not helped by the sands of sin in the machine of progress. Our talk should be of history's hopes and op-portunities, not its tainted motives and dangerous shoals.[2]

Some historical perspective is helpful. Early American revolutionaries felt the same sense of righteousness about the cause against England, and pulpits provided their full share of theological accreditation for colonists clipping the umbilical cord. However, it is instructive to remember that the same revolutionaries, with some self-insight into their own vulner-ability to temptation, built into the fabric of the new govern-ment legislative, executive and judicial checks and balances. We need this same kind of sobriety about the dangers of unrestrained power for our latter-day American revolutions. As the forces of dissent and innovation flex their newly dis-covered muscles and form their new institutions, they too are not exempt from the corruptions attendant to historical momentum. We shall do little service to them by talking only of lassitude. And while their quest must be celebrated as an embodiment of God's mission in the world, and

and even a foretaste of the Kingdom which breaks into time, there must be serious reminders, as well, of the peril of new growth. Here the Christian conscience must play its classical role of participant critic; it gives its heart to the movement but not its soul. Deeply involved, it nonetheless maintains its freedom to dissent and serves the movement as "critic-in-residence." Supporting the forward surge, it provides both accelerator and brake, applying each when the time calls for it.

An example of this kind of "yes, but" relationship to emerging power is the partnership the Christian community can establish with the biological revolutionaries. There had better be some sober Niebuhrians at the council tables of the biotechnicians who will be deciding policy on the creation, control, extension and termination of human life. Christian realists will have on their agenda the goal of affirming the rights of those whose lives will be affected by these developments to have a say in their implementation, especially those of "low degree." And there will be a constant realist surveillance of decision-making procedures, their speed, beneficiaries and democratization.

The revolutions of the young and the black represent other barricades which will be manned by the visionary realist. He will be there to support the student struggling to disperse power in his institution and wrest from the hands of autocracies the control over his own destiny in war and peace. And to balance the vast concentrations of white power in Western society he will be a supporter of black power, as a political, economic and social tool for justice. But he will resist mightily, as well, a hegemony of the young and the black which seeks to excise other partners in the human community. He will be particularly sensitive to the frustration and despair over a stonehearted establishment that breeds these measures of desperation, and penitent for his own participation in the conditions that call them into being. But unchallenged power, even of the righteous, is the pretense of housing an absolute whose home is at the end of history and not in it. The visionary realist cannot be party to that illusion. He will challenge it for the sake of the movement itself, as well as in response to its biblical authenticity, for megalomania brings in its wake the ultimate frustration of the very aims that fathered the cause.

Sobered Expectations

We have been dwelling so far on realism's estimate of the vulnerability of power, and the need for balancing inordinate expressions of it. But there is a broader application, much used by Niebuhr in counsel to his contemporaries about what tomorrow may bring. Do not expect the Kingdom to come in history. Evil grows with good. The anti-Christ appears in the last days. In this rich metaphor Niebuhr saw the ambiguity of all historical achievement. Niebuhr put the stress on the fact that evil persists as society advances, because of the high visibility of the totalitarianisms, tragic wars and depressions of his time. It can easily be forgotten, as we have noted, that he also pointed to history's possibilities. Men can hope for the correction of specific abuses that mar a given period. Within Niebuhr's framework, King had a right to dream that black and white children would walk the streets together in peace.

But Niebuhr was concerned to see that we have no illusions about the next level of historical achievement. That terrain is mined and we must walk gingerly. Not only do those bursting with new hope need this kind of counsel to save them from the despair that comes when tomorrow appears with its disappointments (or the fanaticism grows which refuses to acknowledge the weaknesses of tomorrow), but all people have to prepare themselves for the nightmares. This is a particular necessity for futurists to remember. Moderns who focus on horizons tend to visualize the more sunny prospects. For the realistic visionaries the future is signaled by neither a question mark nor exclamation point. It is an interrobang, the new printer's symbol that blends the two (‽)—an open future, full of exciting promise but interlaced with the possibilities of peril.

The other side of sobriety is the openness to self-criticism. To be schooled in Niebuhr is to know that our plans and projects are infected with our private agendas and molded by our historical location. There must always be room for improvement and revision. No human venture is above criticism, and therefore all must remain open to the future. This motif has its roots in Niebuhr's anthropology. It has links as well to his eschatological commitments. History moves toward its finale. In this tilt forward nothing is solidly nailed down. And as one fixes upon the vision of the future, he is also prepared to take with less than seriousness and a certain good humor all of our pretensions to finality.

Violence and Nonviolence

Is Niebuhr's criticism of pacifism still valid for today's Christian visionaries? Does commitment to shalom mean that, right now, we beat swords into plowshares and refuse to take part in anything that smacks of violence?

Realism does have something to say to the dreamer. But it does so taking into full account the new contexts in which it finds itself. (The latter sensitivity to changing circumstances is "realism" in the more general sense of the term: acknowledgment of the realities of the situation, and implementing goals in the light of them. This awareness is the pragmatic factor in Niebuhrian thought. We have used the term "realism" throughout in the narrower sense: acknowledging the reality of a stubborn evil that persists in the will, behavior and social structures of men.) Those contexts include the development of nuclear weaponry and its increasingly widespread availability, or potential availability, not only to nations but to other groups (paramilitary units within nations, criminal syndicates, etc.), the emergence of new nations with their bursting of colonial bonds and their resistance to neo-colonialism, a straining forward within nations of the Third World to be free of dependence upon the First and Second Worlds, and the growing importance in domestic struggles of tactical and moral questions having to do with nonviolence, defensive violence and aggressive violence. With these and other factors distinguishing the Niebuhrian era from the decade ahead, the following seem to be some implications of realism for visionaries:

1. Given the nuclear arsenal of the major powers and the possible imminent acquisition of comparable resources by other groups, the chance of atomic holocaust becomes even more of a possibility than at present. Adding a particularly fearful dimension to this prospect is the accidental triggering of Armageddon, given the increasingly wide dissemination of these ultimate instruments. Here realism and vision meet. Sinful men with this kind of awesome power in their hands can only be dealt with by concerted effort to beat their missilelike spears into pruning hooks. A nuclear pacifism will mean at the very least radical mutual disarmament proposals and action. It must also produce imaginative war control plans such as the Kurtz surveillance system, which takes into account the realities of national self-interest, and the need for the latent violence of a peacekeeping force, but blends it with visionary hope.[3] Further, given the universal concern about nuclear decimation, it may even mean a mandate for unilateral disarmament, an act comparable to the nonviolent strategy of King which rubbed raw the conscience of a society which could see no way out of disaster unless it responded in kind. In any case, the realist of the seventies can no longer rest comfortably with his balance-of-terror theories; he may be driven by his own presuppositions to put around his neck the same shalom sign worn by the visionary.

2. Many realists marched in the same demonstrations as ideological pacifists because they agree with Niebuhr about the Vietnam war and others like it that hover on the horizon. Where there appears that strange mix of American arrogance

and innocence, political miscalculation and cold-blooded militarism, that leads toward other Vietnams, realists will join visionaries in singing, "All we are saying is give peace a chance."

3. But vision will not erase realism's hardheaded acknowledgement of the role of violence in international affairs. Given "immoral man and even more immoral society," there will have to be, in the foreseeable future, a military component in the settlement of world problems. Hopefully, it can be voluntarized, democratized, internationalized (UN peace-keeping force), its instruments stringently limited (the outlawing of chemical and biological as well as nuclear warfare), strict canons developed on the treatment of civilians, and all these restraints and changes given machinery of enforcement.

4. So far we have been dealing with international conflict. What about domestic warfare? What about the overthrow of tyranny, as in the case of the American Revolution and the revolutions for justice in the Third World?

If the choice is between public peace and order under the eye of a tyrant, and the revolution of the dispossessed and smothered, then realism must remind ideological pacifists that we are faced with the perennial question of the lesser of two evils, and therefore violence cannot be ruled out a priori. Each case must be decided on its merits. As we are talking about vision and realism within the setting of the faith community, Christian communal reflection on the case under question is an important resource for decision-making.

Factors to be taken into account include:

a. Whether there is any chance within the structures and the community's conscience to redress grievances by non-violent political, social or economic action—from the voting booth to sit-in, strike, boycott, demonstration or civil disobedience.

b. Whether violence is counter-productive: in a particular ethos it may encourage the opposition to deepen its resistance, and perhaps to arm itself more extensively, or give greater power to the institutionalized forms of violence.

c. Whether the protesters have so little capacity to effect change by violence that airy schemes and romantic rhetoric invite an even greater despair and potential withdrawal from the struggle when the facts are faced.

d. Whether the contemplated revolution is carried out in a society in which sophisticated weaponry could escalate it into something close to nuclear war, or nuclear war itself.

e. Whether the poverty, hunger and oppression have reached such a point that the death of countless people and the foundations of society can be risked on the chance that the revolt will accomplish its aims. There are dedicated and astute Christian thinkers and activists who believe that in some contexts such risks must be taken, since the way of violent revolution is the lesser of two evils. For some articulate commentary from within just such a context see Colin Morris' *Unyoung, Uncolored, Unpoor.*[4]

f. To these pragmatic considerations the Christian realist must also add the question of whether the ideologies of revolution will in fact institute a society that will be more humane than the present one, and whether the fundamental presuppositions of that revolution are commensurate with basic Christian understandings of the nature and destiny of man.

5. The above discussion has dealt with antiestablishment violence. Realism has some continuing wisdom, too, about establishment instruments of violence, domestic in nature, and specifically the police. Visionaries of all sorts tend to see "blue power" as a prime enemy, front-line guardian of the status quo and active troops of aggression as well. Both the Southern sheriff's deputy and the Northern patrol car have given enough ammunition (literally) for these kinds of charges. But the instruments of domestic law and order cannot (let us put it modestly), in the foreseeable future, be eliminated. Some bounds must be set to the potential anarchy that self-aggrandizement will create if there is no such "force," as the city of Montreal discovered in 1969 when its police went on strike. Again, a visionary like Martin

Luther King, Jr., was a sober enough realist also to seek out the protection of police, the National Guard, and Justice Department agents for civil rights marchers and workers. Without the presence of this latent force the protest movement would not have had its historic impact in South or North.

But vision will not let realism rest content with the status quo. It will work ceaselessly for a democraticized, decently paid and humanized team of peace-keepers. There is evidence of such a breed in the unarmed British bobby, who is not identified even by the most militant European demonstrators as a "pig" but as a firm but fair enemy. And vision will join realism in resisting inordinate powers given to the police, and the ominous police state that lurks in the wings of such developments.

6. Less sophisticated and very real debate about violence goes on in the barroom, newspaper office, kitchen and hunting lodge. It is common in the ghetto and suburbia. It revolves around gun laws, police treatment of militant blacks, black fears of white night riders, horror of both black and white about the rhetoric of violence from left and right, and the anxiety of all about criminal assault. Are vision and realism resources in this common conversation too?

Both make a contribution in the distinction between aggressive and defensive violence. Aggressive violence in the common day-to-day affairs of men is an act that is so clear a breach of shalom that the visionary finds it unthinkable. And realism would add that it is so disruptive of the social fabric that for survival purposes alone the community cannot tolerate it.

Defensive violence, however, in which the home or headquarters of social change agents is under physical threat, is a counsel of prudence the realist must teach the visionary, especially in violence-prone locales. Anyone who has slept in a civil rights center in the midst of a Southern voter registration drive knows the importance of public knowledge of the shotgun leaning against the wall. And Northern black militants have declared their right to self-defense as loudly as any surburban housewife fearful of the marauder portrayed on late-night TV.

Here, again, the context is important. In a relatively civilized society where there is public disapproval of guns and violent encounters, realism would agree with vision that the Deacons for Defense would hardly be a missionary endeavor. Where there is such an ethos, and therefore the possibility of giving up devices that are inherently antishalom, then every effort should be made to aid and abet citizen peacemaking. But where primitive Wild-West gun-toting is the virtual premise of a hate-ridden society, and no protection can be guaranteed by the so-called law and order forces, then the citizens, and we are thinking here of the creative change agents in particular, must exercise their right to defend themselves, as a lesser evil than the loss of loved ones, life, limb and cause. Let it be clear also that in a totalitarian society, the right to defense of people and cause may well include the "aggressive" action of a Bonhoeffer plot against a Hitler.[5]

Dialectical Dreaming

Realism must be around to water the heady wines of the new visionary. But while realism must fight for its say in programs of ecclesiastical and secular action, it will not want that action reduced to only the limited dreams sketched above. Somewhere, somehow, as Niebuhr himself affirmed, there must be a small cadre of those who will lift up and embody the purest of visions. Such a community of conscience reminds us that anything less than the Kingdom is less than God's final intent for his world. It forces us to realize that our translations, qualifications and scaling down of this ultimate dream of perfection are always to be lured toward and judged by the historically marginal perfectionist.

For the rest of us who cannot or choose not to live along the edges of historical action, but who believe nonetheless that shalom is in a crucial way the reference point for those who live in the mainstream, there must be another way. Let us call it dialectical dreaming. It is a Yes and No to the actualizing right now of shalom. It marries realism to hope. It produces practical visionaries or, more exactly, penitent visionaries. They press toward the Goal but know they must settle regularly for less. And because they are visionaries, the conscience rubbed raw by that compromise is almost unbearable. The lure of the vision and the pain of its breach drives them harder toward the Goal. The sting of their guilt is made livable by the divine forgiveness. But dream they will, and the accent will be on the possibilities rather than the impossibilities of history, hope rather than hopelessness, grace more than sin, resurrection overcoming crucifixion.

We have been treating realism and vision as opposite themes which somehow have to learn to live with each other, and that is basically so. However, there is in a certain sense a unity, at least in the design of Christian faith. The biblical dream knows that it is, in the final analysis, a dream. Biblical visionaries nurse no illusions about man's ability to catch the dream in the nets of his history. Although we are moved by faith to struggle toward it, and by hope to celebrate its fragmentary happenings, we are indeed still pilgrims moving toward it, but remain strangers to it. The Christian visionary is therefore, by definition, a realist. He knows that he is set down in a society that is radically out of kilter. That gap, between what is and what ought to be, fires him to action toward the Future, but it also saves him from the debilitating despair of the idealist who is unprepared for the shock of reality. Christian vision, at its deepest level, *is* Christian realism.

V

Large Promise, Small Perils

      Christian realism by no means exhausts the Niebuhrian bequest to the future. The legacy runs from somber warnings for the smug and complacent to insights on laughter for the dour and depressed. It ranges over counsel for the left and the right, the church and the world, the mystic and the secular. The promissory motifs in this assorted wisdom, all of which go back to basic Niebuhrian postulates about man and God, we shall attempt to identify in this chapter.

But Niebuhr is no all-wise guru, as he is the first to admit. Some of his notions are mistaken, askew, dated. Critics he has aplenty. Therefore in good Niebuhrian style we shall first attend to the perils of our subject. But departing therefrom, we shall find more to celebrate than denigrate. What else, for a book by a partisan on "the promise of Reinhold Niebuhr"?

It is not hard to find the critics and criticisms. They surface irately in the wake of his attacks on the illusions of modern man. Each target of his lightning hurls back his own bolts. Marxists accuse him of being an apologist for capitalism. The right wing calls him a communist. Naturalists declare that he wallows in religious superstition. Idealists assert that he has sold out to irrationalism. Pacifists bewail his compromise with the absolutes of love. Cynics claim that he confuses action with his high principles. Orthodox Christians label him as an unbeliever who fails to hew the line on everything from the divinity of Christ and the resurrection to the doctrine of the Holy Spirit. The church-minded feel he ignores the institution, or criticizes it too much. The worldly say he is too churchy. The pious declare that he is too political. The political say he is too pious.

Amid the wild charges against Niebuhr of one or another gored ox, there are some that do strike home. Niebuhr's doctrine of the church is undeveloped, and his place for the Holy Spirit is indeed minimal. Nature does get smothered by history. He is not a systematic theologian. Neither is he a painstaking philosopher. His tendency to portray options in broad brush strokes lends itself to classifying the opposition too easily and dismissing it too brusquely. He has made some serious political miscalculations.

While we might profitably elaborate each of these, our limited space suggests that we choose rather to concentrate on several other criticisms that seem of particular importance in the current forum of theological debate and social concern.

Man's Coming of Age

Dietrich Bonhoeffer has helped a generation of Christians to see at least two things about the process of secularization:

1. Religious belief has been gradually edged out of the role of problem solver. Secular men increasingly turn to secular means when they want protection from, or control of, the storms in their atmosphere, society, and soul. A religion that locates God only in those places not yet fathomed by man, or doing tasks yet undone by man—a "god of the gaps"—is doomed. Man's maturation gives him the present power and future promise of closing those fissures.

2. Christian faith celebrates this coming of age. God is the kind of Father who wants grown-up sons that make it on their own. God is not to be treated as a "deus ex machina" (the helpful divinity dropped down on the stage at a critical

moment in ancient theater) who rushes to bail us out of difficulties for which we ourselves should assume responsibility. He is not a "Big Daddy" whose paternalism or autocracy keeps his children dependent. As the early church worked out an understanding of Jesus (at the councils of Nicaea and Chalcedon) which affirmed that in this full and free human God himself was also present, so this paradox suggests a Father, who frees his children for their own future, yet expresses his own paternal grace in, with and under man's self-determination.

For some it will need to be said that the race's coming of age is not moral maturity. Bonhoeffer was no misty-eyed perfectionist. He knew that evil grows with good. Coming of age is the maturing of historical capacity and possibility, a new facility which can be corrupted at every level of achievement. But the point here is that man's "making it" without benefit of clergy is God's doing.

The Passing of the God of the Gaps. Reinhold Niebuhr's polemics against the options of modernity tended to position him awkwardly for the appropriation of these theses. He saw that the going secular analyses of man were manifestly wrong. The biblical answers made much more sense. From that it was a short step to the claim that only those who made the act of faith had access to fundamental truths about the human situation. At the height of Niebuhr's career this kind of apologetic was a familiar one.

But if it is only biblical faith that can equip men for living a serene yet responsible life, then mankind can make it only with "Big Daddy." Religion, edged off its turf by an advancing science, yet holds one more card: it alone can save men from complacency and arrogance, on the one hand, and despair and self-forgetfulness, on the other. This is "god of the gap" thinking. It declines to cut the apron strings. To believe in a God who wills man's coming of age is to be ready to acknowledge that secular men with secular savvy might be able to avoid the Scylla of pretension and Charybdis of

[83]

escape. And it is to encourage him to do it, and to celebrate that fact when he does.

There are suggestions of this in Niebuhr throughout his work in such notions as general revelation, the acknowledgments of hints of ultimate meaning in secular experience, his appreciation for the insights of such thinkers as Marx and Freud, and the declaration that Christian wisdom about man can be validated inductively. And increasingly so in his later writings, he spoke of the importance of secular sources as well as secular confirmation of fundamental knowledge about man, abandoning the Christian code language of original sin for more generally understandable descriptions, such as "man's self-regarding impulses." But the main burden of his apologetic has always tended to be the thesis that faith is a necessary companion for the negotiation of the human pilgrimage, for it makes much better sense of the heights and depths of human life than alternative perspectives.

Bonhoeffer's discernment of the significance of secularization, and his own Christian secularity, are correctives to the triumphalist note in Neibuhr's apologetic. But an uncritical secularity is no better than a mindless neo-orthodoxy. Something of Niebuhr's insight into the supportive role of faith can be incorporated into the maturation motifs. Thus: while it is ideally possible and biblically urgent for man to manage his own future with secular wisdom—and modern advances give increasing evidence of this capacity—coming of age is a painfully slow process. History is organism as well as artifact, as Niebuhr regularly affirms, and Christian secularity can make the same mistake as the old voluntarism, which assumed too easily that the future could be contrived by human ingenuity. A father with his zeal to encourage maturity in his son yet comes to his assistance when that son faces burdens that outpace growth. A God who wills his world's majority will give no less gifts than his earthly counterpart to support children not yet come of age. Among these resources may well be the instincts and insights of "high religion." Thus biblical wisdom about human nature is a crucial resource on man's pilgrimage, as Niebuhr says. But it is provisional, the work of a tutor whose goal is a self-starting student. It forswears the encouragement of dependency and waving the flags of triumphalism, accepting the limited role of catalyst of a wisdom God brings, not only through special measures but through his secular grace.

The Love of God for His Own Sake. To relinquish a defense of faith based on the latter's claim to cope more effectively with life's ambiguities may force us to come to terms with another dimension of faith often neglected by the pragmatic Western mentality. Actually, echoes of it can be heard in Niebuhr's writings. I believe its notes must be sounded with particular clarity in an era of rapid secularization of religious functions. And, its accents will be understood by the "counter-culture" of the young who gravitate toward a neomysticism.

Niebuhr remarked from time to time upon the paradox that the most productive things often come not by prudence and calculation but when they are unintended. And he believed this kind of heedlessness to be at the center of Christian belief. The central understandings in Christian faith about man can be appropriated only by self-abandonment and penitence. Faith is not heavenly hedonism but the love of God for his own sake. This "for its own sake" dimension is an important one in an era of secularization, for it is the other side of our mandate to celebrate the coming-of-age process. We are liberated to affirm secularization because the truth of our fundamental convictions and commitments does not finally rest on its pragmatic value. Through and beyond its usefulness to man's struggle to be human—a test that must always remain in order to disqualify claimants which cannot produce ethical fruits—can be seen a glimpse of a friendship with God that is not justified by utility. It is simply there to be had. God is to be loved because he is God.

Sensitive young people today, expressing their revulsion with our empirical, pragmatic, secular society, its technological horrors and calculating egoism, are flirting with the Oriental and the esoteric. Niebuhr notes the periodic slide of rationalism into mysticism. We may well be seeing that rhythm once again. His warnings about the possibility of anti-intellectualism and a retreat inward and away from historical responsibility in such a swing of the pendulum have to be taken seriously. However, in this shift there is an authentic judgment on the life of self-interested calculation, the hypocrisies of an affluent society, and a sound instinct for the inscrutable, too easily exorcised by a cocksure scientism. And Niebuhr himself spoke movingly of mystery as integral to faith, taking to task the insensitivity of the death-of-God theologians to this dimension. Perhaps odd talk of a life with God which has no agendas may find resonance among those who search for deeper things.

Humor and Faith

Celebration, play, humor and laughter are being rediscovered in the religious community. Christ grins out at us from the illustration of a *Playboy* article by Harvey Cox, who argues there, and in *The Feast of Fools*, the importance of festivity and fantasy. Others plead *For God's Sake Laugh!* and bring together anthologies of *Holy Laughter*. [1] The mood is reflected in celebrative worship that makes full use of the sounds of folk and rock, the sights of banners, balloons and multimedia techniques, and smells of incense.

Well before such festive goings-on, when sobriety was the order of the day in both worship and theology, Reinhold Niebuhr was reminding us that the God "who sits in the heavens laughs." (Psalm 2:4). In some reflections of the mid-forties, widely read and reprinted, he explored the intriguing kinship of humor and faith. What he had to say about that relationship probes it more deeply than much of the current crop of comment on the religious significance of drollery.

Hope and happiness blend as in the art of Corita Kent. So it is predictable that theologies of hope will find themselves very much at home in the midst of festive color and celebrative sound. Niebuhr too, as an ultimate hoper (a submerged motif as we have noted, given the historical context of his labors), also spoke of a joy commensurate with the final overcoming of the power of evil and, in individual terms, "on the other side of the experience of penitence." But faith strikes its note of triumph (Niebuhr thinks of it more often as serenity than gaiety) only after passing through a shadowy valley. The note of crucifixion of self, society and God is not greatly in evidence in today's theologies of play and celebration. The same absence is notable in their liturgical counterparts. "Is folk music stuck on a single note?" asks a perceptive critic who finds many efforts at contemporary worship lacking in depth and verging on the sentimental.[2]

Niebuhr has a sharp eye for these profundities and finds laughter helpless to deal with them. The depths of our own self-will and the heights of our pretension, the incongruity of death, the malice that exterminates six million Jews and bludgeons a small Asian nation are no laughing matter. To these grim facts only penitence, faith and sacrificial love are fit responses. Laughter in the face of these realities is gallows humor, bitter and self-defeating.

Other depth dimensions also deserve better than a genial grin. One of them is the mystery of the divine life and action, manifest centrally in the cross. Although direct quotation has been purposely avoided in this volume in the interests of a free-flowing interpretation of the promissory, we cite here a passage which not only illustrates the point under discussion but also uncovers a basic theological foundation in Niebuhr's thought.

There is ... no humour in the scene of Christ upon the cross ... because the justice and mercy of God are fully revealed in it. In that revelation God's justice is made the more terrible because the sin of man is disclosed in its full dimension. It is rebellion against God

from which God Himself suffers. God cannot remit the consequences of sin; yet He does show mercy by taking the consequences
upon and into Himself. This is the main burden of the disclosure of
God in Christ. This is the final clue to the mystery of the divine
character.[3]

Faith alone can deal with the ultimate mysteries. But there
is plenty of room for laughter in dealing with the penultimate
ones. Niebuhr tells us that the medicine for the sickness of
petty self-inflation is a sense of humor that learns not to take
ourselves so seriously. The same laughter is proper judgment
on the pretensions of others. Both we and they fail to see the
incongruity between our conceits and our mediocrity. And
laughter is a good resource in coming to terms with many
other juxtapositions with which we must learn to live, such as
the unpredictable events that intrude upon our well-laid
plans, and the irrationalities that mar our dreams.

The kinship between humor and faith lies precisely at the
point of dealing with the incongruities of our life, our pretension and our performance, our sublime expectations and the
modest and often fractured realities, our greatness and our
weakness. Laughter plays its role in dealing with these ill fits,
as does faith. Their jurisdictions and interrelationship are set
forth in a simple passage that illustrates not only an insight
but also the kind of purple patch to be found not infrequently in this powerful writer: "there is laughter in the
vestibule of the temple, the echo of laughter in the temple
itself, but only faith and prayer, and no laughter, in the holy
of holies."[4]

Advice for the Right and the Left

Political Reaction and Its Priests. In a decade which shows
signs of growing backlash and retrenchment, Niebuhr's
running battle with political and religious reactionaries of
another day offers many lessons. Warnings about the pride of
nation, race and class are anything but obsolete. Militarism

and chauvinism ally themselves today with a confused idealism to wage war, support military juntas and resist movements for reform on several continents. Meanwhile the same forces harass and imprison the young dissenter in this country. White racism, cut from the same cloth as old blood-and-soil philosophies, gains momentum in South and North, at home and abroad. A conscienceless majority strives to protect its affluence, resists programs for the poverty-ridden, and greets the lament of the urban poor and the dissenter with its own cries of "law and order."

These are familiar sounds. We have to do with themes vigorously underscored by Niebuhr: the ubiquity of self-regard, its demonic compounding in the theater of historical forces, its special arrogance among the powerful, and the self-righteous smoke screen which such proud power always lays down around itself. Out of this comes the mandate, as fresh as ever, to challenge, disperse and balance this new imperialism of the right.

The political right is matched in its pretension by the religious right. In fact the two become bedfellows in a new civil religion in which old flirtations of the fifties between pietism and complacency reach their consummation in a White House chapel which comes under Niebuhr's sharp attack.[5] The union is so firm that an old pietism that drew back from involvement in politics now baptizes the programs of the powers that be, dispenses absolution for their conscience, and excommunicates from the body politic itself the young, the black and the poor who reject the doctrinal line. Niebuhr's misgivings about Billy Graham and Norman Vincent Peale, declared in the midst of the postwar religious boom, are expressed again at the outset of "the Nixon era" and will have perennial significance whenever a religion of cheap grace provides cover for political reaction.

But Niebuhr will be no one's uncritical ally. Both left and right need to hear a word that shakes their certainties and presumed righteousness. We have spoken about the need for realism on the part of the oppressed who now flex their muscles and surge forward to claim their inheritance. Their motives are also mixed and their new power not impervious to corruption. Niebuhr's insight into Marxist utopianism and its consequences are of particular importance in a time of new dialogue and of simplistic anticapitalist slogans and dreams of the New Left. But we concentrate here on some less obvious Niebuhrian correctives.

The Minutes of the Last Meeting. One of them is Niebuhr's historical sense. He believes, in the words of a college chaplain, that "We can avoid a lot of nonsense by reading the minutes of the last meeting." Much of his political analysis was fashioned from the data of the past. A generation that is mesmerized by the present and thinks that the Now has no lessons to learn from the Then is throwing away one of its most valuable tools for social change. The present is no simple repetition of the "once upon a time," but neither is it discontinuous with it. Niebuhr understood historical novelty but was aware as well of its continuities, and harnessed this understanding to the task of political action.

We shall speak more later of the value of understanding faith's heritage as well as the world's past. There is, however, a component in the religious community that parallels the lack of historical sense in secular movements, which deserves mention among the aberrations of the left. That is the radical morality. Situation ethics carries on its own campaign against Niebuhr for his "ontological" rather than his "existential" ethics, protesting an absolute that stands embarrassingly over each action, causing "remorse" when breached.

We have examined Niebuhr's affirmation of the Kingdom of God as the final standard by which all our lesser motives, actions and structures must be judged, and toward which they must aspire, albeit under the limiting conditions of sin and finitude. To remove this ultimate Ought against which we are called to measure our movements is not only to censor the final chapter in the Christian story; it also provides a handy religious confirmation of the easy conscience of modern man, glad to be told by some Christian ethicists that he need not be burdened with guilt feelings when party to some hurt to others, done, presumably, out of benevolence. Thus the case of the British intelligence staff in World War II: "When they let a number of women agents return to Germany to certain arrest and death in order to keep secret the fact that they had broken the German code. Situational casuistry could easily approve their decision."[6] Here, Niebuhr the "dreamer," who refuses to eliminate the trans-historical vision, must call into question the simple equation between what must be done and what is ultimately right. For him, choices that fly in the face of the sacrificial love of the Kingdom are not decisions man ought to be able to "easily approve." They are *hard* choices, made, whichever way, in fear and trembling, in penitence for the evil done, even though it be the lesser evil, and with a plea for divine forgive-ness. And, too, the chooser is driven by a vision to work all the harder toward a world of peace where such decisions will not have to be made.

The captivity to the existential Now in situation ethics must also be underscored. That Now surely must affect our decision-making. But this slender moment of time does not exhaust the data. Realism is well aware of the distortions introduced by that limited immediate situational perspective, and aggravated by its self-interest. We need whomever we can get at the council tables of decision, and that includes both the fathers and the brethren. Input comes from the historic experience of the race, and from the research done by the covenant community in which the chooser lives. The rugged individualism and exclusive present-orientation of situation ethics must be corrected by the community's moral lore, history's wisdom and a corporate style of decision-making.

To take seriously the general consensus points on moral conduct in Christian tradition and in the experience of the race does not mean we treat them as absolute and eternal. They are, indeed, historically conditioned, but they are important corporate research data on what makes and keeps life human. As such, they are not rigid law, laid down from above, but come as counsel and guidelines to a generation that rightfully does not accept things on the authority of autocrats.

But that same generation knows that no man is an island. Moral decision-making must be made somewhere in range of the mainland of human community and, for the Christian, also the faith community. To take the community into serious account includes, of course, the present task of updating and translating, the development of "middle axioms" and guidelines on questions for which there is no historic research; let us say, the creation, control and indefinite extension of human life now on the drawing board and even in the laboratories of the life sciences. Not moral Lone Rangers but community inquiry and emerging guidelines are needed for *aggiornamento* in ethics. The need for this kind of corporate quest is itself a lesson learned from the past experience of the faith community.

The Way of Doing Theology

Reflection in the Context of Involvement. Christian education experts gather in Chicago for their annual meeting to hear welfare mothers "tell it like it is," visit a packing-house workers' meeting, participate in a demonstration of seminary students. Ministers take a plunge on the skid rows of the city with $2 in their pockets and the mandate to make it on their own for two days in urban centers around the country. Seminaries develop a "curriculum of the seventies" which exposes the student to the victims and structures of power in the modern world as he studies his Augustine and St. Paul. This "action research" in the church traces its immediate lineage to the life and thought of Dietrich Bonhoeffer. He laid the groundwork for the social existentialism of Gibson Winter, Harvey Cox, and the World Council of Churches' Missionary Structure Study. These in turn helped to shape the emphasis on social involvement as the context for "doing theology."

[92]

Long before this "new" learning methodology captured the imagination of churchmen, Reinhold Niebuhr was living out the action-reflection rhythm. Alexander Miller, one of the British thinkers influenced by Niebuhr, who walked his own picket lines in the thirties and forties, put it this way: "The safest place for the theologian is in the midst of the social struggle."

One of the ironies in the life-style of our irony-conscious subject is his frequent disclaimer that he is really a theologian because of his preoccupation with social action, and his apology that he should have spent more time at his desk and less in political movements. Now any academic or Sunday School pupil content to sit in the classroom and spin out talk about Jesus, devoid of companionship with the worldly Christ who meets us in our ministry to the sick, the poor, the hungry, the prisoner (Matthew 25), is seen to be starving himself theologically and spiritually. Christ teaches about himself at those points in the human ferment where he is at work. To know him we must be there. Niebuhr's critique of perfectionism, his understanding of pride, the ambiguity of the righteous, idolatry, Old Testament prophetism, the need for forgiveness, the reality of the hidden Christ and many other themes are directly related to his participation in the crunch of political and social life. His example has taught a generation where theology must be done and should set the same pace for those to come.

The Secular Dialogue. From his first confrontations with Marx and Freud to his review of the latest book on political thought or psychological theory, Niebuhr has carried on an appreciative yet critical conversation with nonecclesiastical thought. The giants, and some of the midgets too, of the human community were not just set up as targets for thunderbolts from on high (he surely hurled his fair share), but as partners in the intellectual pilgrimage whose insights were to be taken seriously and honored for their truth.

In his later writing Niebuhr accented his debt to secular

thought. And he attempted to translate more simply into general human categories some of his understandings about human nature and destiny. These themes are highlighted in *Man's Nature and His Communities* (1965), but there are traces of this Christian secularity from the beginning of his career. The "hidden Christ" at work in the thoughts and perspectives of wise men outside the covenant stream was a constant in his reflections. Their wisdom serves to supplement, clarify and implement the insights of the Christian community. God raises up children of Abraham from the secular stones.

The Christian Story. In an era of the decline of books of sermons, Niebuhr's collections of sermons (*Beyond Tragedy* and *Discerning the Signs of the Times*) are still widely read. In these volumes, but also in his more scholarly works and even in his political editorials, Old and New Testament passages often provided the springboard for reflection. Niebuhr took the Christian story seriously. Involvement, yes; secular savvy, yes. But they came to be, or to be acknowledged, because of fundamental commitments to the biblical tale.

The Storybook: Life with the Story means at least two basic things. For one, familiarity with the Bible. Niebuhr frequently does his theology in conversation with the biblical text. Among those passages to which allusion is frequently made are the tower of Babel story, honest Pauline perceptions such as "the good that I would, I do not, and that which I would not, I do" and "I know nothing against myself but he who judges me is the Lord," Peter's affirmation of his final loyalty, "We must obey God and not men," the Psalmist's description of God's grandeur and man's historical folly, "He that sitteth in the heavens shall laugh: the Lord shall have them in derision," and the Christian's final assurance, "nothing can separate us from the love of God." Millions of Sunday morning worshipers during the forties and fifties discovered dimensions of pride in man and laughter in God of which they had never heard in a pre-Niebuhrian era. Unfamiliar texts became regular fare by way of a generation of preaching influenced by Niebuhrian insights.

Conversation with the Bible is not biblicism. Niebuhr was accused of that sometimes by agnostic friends whose only exposure to faith was quotation-spouting Sunday morning radio evangelists. His biblical thunder sounded similar, but careful listeners were aware of the critical scholarship through which the Storybook had passed to get at the grist. But more important, what really interested Niebuhr in his expositions were the "myths." Here were the nuggets. They had to be refined to get the gold, of course—that's what Niebuhr's preaching and teaching were all about. The truth about the ambiguity of the human condition, the corruptions of the good and the possibilities of history were traced out in the Genesis account, the Babel tale, and the death and resurrection of Christ.

The Storytellers: It is possible to be absorbed in the Story lines of the Book but pay little attention to fellow Storytellers, the second crucial way the word gets out. That is our Protestant problem. Not so Niebuhr. He drew the conversation circle wide enough to include both the fathers and the brethren. Niebuhr listened to and argued with Augustine, Luther, Thomas, Kierkegaard. They found their way into many a footnote which provided more scrupulous professional historians a chance to comment on Niebuhr's use or misuse of his sources. All of which widened the dialogue even further.

Niebuhr's exchanges with contemporary Christian thinkers went on concurrently with the classic theologians. Participation in the World Council of Churches and its predecessor ecumenical agencies brought Niebuhr into debate with the giants of his time. We have spoken about the sharp exchange with Barth in connection with the 1948 Assembly. His colleagues on the Union faculty, such as Paul Tillich and John Bennett, offered him a constant chance to sharpen his insights. And his wide-ranging speaking tours brought him into contact with the keenest theological minds of the day.

Christian realism is not eremite theology. It was shaped by a life together in the theological fraternity, and within a larger Christian community.

Courage to Change

This title of June Bingham's biography of Niebuhr, taken from his famous prayer, puts the finger on this last quality of the Niebuhrian style, openness to the future. One of the marks of a great theologian is his capacity to develop, at the painful price of admitting mistakes, abandoning old categories, moving along new frontiers.

An allied quality of an open theologian is his ability to discern the signs of the times and speak the right word in and to these times. When the Nazi era pleaded for a prophetic indictment and a shattering of sentimental illusions, Niebuhr stood up to speak his piece. When there appeared a pietism which professed to know all about human sin but did not have its vision stretched to serve its Lord in the structures of the common life, it was Niebuhr who rebuked a Billy Graham while many in the officialdom of the church acclaimed his New York revival. When social-action types collapsed the Gospel into an attack on economic and political structures, he spoke about the need for prayer and the broken self. When "secularism" became a favorite swearword, Niebuhr underscored the common grace at work in nonecclesiastical persons and movements. When the secular theology took up its refrain, he reminded its adherents of mystery and myth and the grandeur of God. In each of these cases, Niebuhr's thought moves away from theses with which he had become too neatly associated. But while he was prepared to abandon positions found untenable, he also maintained commitments he believed to be of continuing significance.

The courage to change makes for a pilgrim theology. But the traveler must carry a well-stocked pack. Its supplies include provender prepared by others who have gone before and know the sustenance needed for unmarked trails. The pilgrimage goes forward, open to the future but fortified by the past.

The past's provisions served Niebuhr well in his journey through an era that had to be reminded of forgotten things— the biblical wisdom about the sin in man and the tragic in history. Realism was healthy food, and Niebuhr a good guide for having been strengthened by it.

Now on another leg of the journey, the pilgrim reaches into his kit bag and comes up with hope to sustain him. It is an elixir that stirs young men to see visions and old men to dream dreams. Hidden deep down in Niebuhr's knapsack we have discovered some of the same refreshment, too. But alone it is a diet that lacks nourishment for the long haul. The brown bread of realism must balance the heady wines of hope. It is in the Niebuhrian pack this abundant staple is to be found that can keep alive today's visions and tomorrow's dreams. We survive, and make headway on our pilgrimage, with a guide equipped for times of both threat and expectation, a man for all seasons. In that lies the promise of Reinhold Niebuhr.

Notes

Introduction

1. Gordon Harland, *The Thought of Reinhold Niebuhr* (New York: Oxford University Press, 1960); Charles W. Kegley and Robert W. Bretall, editors, *Reinhold Neibuhr: His Religious, Social and Political Thought* (New York: The Macmillan Company, 1956); June Bingham, *Courage to Change: An Introduction to the Life and Thought of Reinhold Niebuhr* (New York: Charles Scribner's Sons, 1961).

Chapter I. The Life and Style of Reinhold Niebuhr

1. Reinhold Niebuhr, "Toward Intra-Christian Endeavors," *The Christian Century,* Vol. LXXXVI, No. 53 (December 31, 1969), p. 1664.

2. Ronald H. Stone, "An Interview with Reinhold Niebuhr," *Christianity and Crisis,* Vol. XXIX, No. 4 (March 17, 1969), pp. 48-52.

3. Richard Shaull, "Theology and the Transformation of Society," *Theology Today,* Vol. XXV, No. 1 (April, 1968), pp. 23-36.

4. John Bennett, Roger L. Shinn et. al., "Christian Realism: A Symposium," *Christianity and Crisis,* Vol. XXVIII, No. 14 (August 5, 1968), pp. 175-190.

Chapter II. Theological Roots

1. Reinhold Niebuhr, *The Nature and Destiny of Man,* Vol. I, p. 3.

Chapter III. Political Shoots

    1. Reinhold Niebuhr, *The Children of Light and the Children of Darkness,* p. xiii.

Chapter IV. Realism and Vision

    1. John Bennett, in "Christian Realism: A Symposium," *loc. cit.,* p. 176.

    2. See Harvey G. Cox, *On Not Leaving It to the Snake* (New York: The Macmillan Company, 1968), especially pp. vii-xviii.

    3. Howard and Harriet Kurtz, "Global Compassionate Power," *Renewal* (June, 1967), pp. 1, 3-17.

    4. Colin Morris, *Unyoung, Uncolored, Unpoor* (New York: Abingdon Press, 1969).

    5. Ibid. Again Colin Morris' reflections are much to the point; see especially pp. 19-34, 82-157.

Chapter V. Large Promise, Small Perils

    1. Harvey G. Cox, *The Feast of Fools* (Cambridge, Mass.: Harvard University Press, 1969); Nevin Vos, *For God's Sake Laugh!* (Richmond, Va.: John Knox Press, 1967); M. Conrad Hyers, Editor, *Holy Laughter* (New York: The Seabury Press, 1969).

    2. "Is Folk Music Stuck on a Single Note?" *National Catholic Reporter,* Vol. 6, No. 8 (December 17, 1969), pp. 1, 7.

    3. Reinhold Niebuhr, "Humour and Faith," in *Discerning the Signs of the Times,* pp. 118-119.

    4. *Ibid.,* p. 131.

    5. Reinhold Niebuhr, "The King's Chapel and the King's Court," *Christianity and Crisis,* Vol. XXIX, No. 14 (August 4, 1969), pp. 211-212.

    6. Joseph Fletcher, *Situation Ethics* (Philadelphia: Westminster Press, 1966), p. 98.

A Selected Bibliography of Works by Reinhold Niebuhr

Does Civilization Need Religion? New York: The Macmillan Company, 1927, 1941.

Leaves from the Notebook of a Tamed Cynic. New York: Willet, Clark and Colby, 1929; World Publishing Company (Meridian Books), 1957.

The Contribution of Religion to Social Work. New York: Columbia University Press, 1932.

Moral Man and Immoral Society. New York and London: Charles Scribner's Sons, 1932, 1960.

Reflections on the End of an Era. New York: Charles Scribner's Sons, 1934.

An Interpretation of Christian Ethics. New York: Harper and Brothers, 1935; World Publishing Company (Meridian Books), 1956, with a new preface by the author, 1963.

Beyond Tragedy. New York: Charles Scribner's Sons, 1937.

Christianity and Power Politics. New York: Charles Scribner's Sons, 1940; Archon, Shoe String Press, 1969.

The Nature and Destiny of Man. Two volumes. New York: Charles Scribner's Sons, 1941, 1943; one-volume edition, 1948, 1953, 1964.

The Children of Light and the Children of Darkness. New York: Charles Scribner's Sons, 1944, 1960.

Discerning the Signs of the Times. New York: Charles Scribner's Sons, 1946.

Faith and History. New York: Charles Scribner's Sons, 1949.

The Irony of American History. New York: Charles Scribner's Sons, 1952, 1958.

Christian Realism and Political Problems. New York: Charles Scribner's Sons, 1953.

The Self and the Dramas of History. New York: Charles Scribner's Sons, 1955.

Love and Justice. Edited by D. B. Robertson, Philadelphia: Westminster Press, 1957; Cleveland: World Publishing Company (Meridian Books), 1967.

The World Crisis and American Responsibility. Collected and edited by Ernest W. Lefever. New York: Association Press, 1958.

Pious and Secular America. New York: Charles Scribner's Sons, 1958.

Essays in Applied Christianity. Selected and edited by D. B. Robertson. New York: World Publishing Company (Meridian Books), 1959.

The Structure of Nations and Empires. New York: Charles Scribner's Sons, 1959.

Reinhold Niebuhr on Politics. Edited by Harry R. Davis and Robert C. Good. New York: Charles Scribner's Sons, 1960.

A Nation So Conceived. With Alan Heimert. New York: Charles Scribner's Sons, 1963.

Man's Nature and His Communities. New York: Charles Scribner's Sons, 1965, 1968.

Faith and Politics. Edited by Ronald H. Stone. New York: George Braziller, 1968.

For a thorough record of the books, essays in collections, articles in periodicals, and book reviews of the author, plus writings about him, up through the year 1953, see D. B. Robertson, *Reinhold Niebuhr's Works: A Bibliography* (Berea, Ky.: The Berea College Press, 1954).